Lava Dawgs
A Fight for Fallujah

By: Charlie Moose

Table of Contents

Author's Note

I began writing this book as a Marine, Infantryman and participant of an epic, urban battle in the heart of Iraq in 2004. I was never a hero, but I have been witness to many of them. I was a volunteer, and it was the best and worst time of my entire life. There are few events, if any, that could ever compare to the nature of close-quarters, urban combat. I was grateful to survive it, when many brave men died or were severely wounded. Admittedly, I was a bit insecure to embark on this journey of the written word because I wasn't sure if I could do justice to the story and the sacrifices that were made. However, I wrote this work, not for money or recognition, but for the lowly, enlisted, grunt Marine who carries a rifle and volunteers to serve something greater than self, at least once in his lifetime.

I would like to thank all those people and fellow Marines who helped make this special project possible. I'd like to specifically thank all my brethren, to include, B. Morales, C. Williamson, A. Hall, K. Kane, J. Brisch, Munoz (Hijo de Mexico), J. Napier, and many other Fallujah Veterans, who submitted stories and helped to recollect information for the material of this book. I also want to recognize and thank R.D. Groves for his contribution to the editing process.

Lastly and certainly not least, I'd like to convey my special thanks and appreciation to my wife, Myrna, for all her technical support, love, and encouragement through this arduous ordeal, despite myself. None of this would have been possible without you.

This book is dedicated to all those Marines, Navy Corpsman, and Soldiers who fought and died in the Battles for Fallujah.

Semper

"This one time, it was all about mysterious places and cammie faces. A different English dialect, like mumbled screams with big eye balls and throbbing jugulars. A musical rhythm with every step and acute peripheral vision. Methodical and ritualistic. Absurd and automatic, but normal and endured. Irony and comic relief were an unsatisfactory justification for the reality of things. Addicted to the possibility of things. Obsessing about the policy of things. But then there were nights that were quiet and cold, with the muffled static of 'Roger, Roger, Check'...and skies that couldn't have been painted by hand, only ambushed by epiphany. At peace with the worst, because that's protocol. Things that cannot be unlearned, but unleashed. Empty eyes, dirty skin...swollen mind, dirty sin. Expunged in the name of Good Will. Ahhhh, but bitter sweet, indeed." - CM

Chapter 1
A Perfect Storm

The sun was high in the sky when the orders came down to dig in on the outskirts of the desert, less than a 'click' (1000 meters) away from the notorious city of Fallujah. The terrain was a no man's land of rocky berms and intensely compacted sand - a seemingly impenetrable surface. All the Marines had were flimsy collapsible grunt shovels called e-tools. After digging only inches into the sunbaked earth, several of the Marines had begun breaking them into pieces just to prove the point.

The Battalion Commander, Lt. Col. Mad Mike, walked the lines. He was short, formal, oddly assertive, ambitious, and well-schooled, but his demeanor leaked a sinister side. "Hey gents, you better get in that ground one way or another. If we start taking indirect mortar fire, you'll be using your finger nails and teeth." The Marines looked around in dismay. "I'm gonna die before I even step foot in this damned city from diggin' these fuckin' rocks, man," said Husker. "It doesn't get hot like this in Nebraska." "Well then hydrate, boot! We ain't outta water yet", roared JD with a sarcastic laugh. Husker referred to himself as "lightly, salted". He was eighteen years old and green behind the ears. He had served less than a year in the Corps before finding himself in combat, on his first deployment.

JD, on the other hand, was old beyond his years at twenty-six. He was prior Army and previously served time in Kosovo. The Marines burrowed into their shallow holes as American fighter jets screeched overhead, dropping their loads. The explosions emitted huge plumes of smoke, fire, and debris into the air before the Marines even heard the blast as the sound traveled through a vacuum. Typically the Marines couldn't see them fly by. Instead, they only lay witness to the concussion of their wrath, upsetting the city skyline. For the Marines, this experience was humbling and surreal. From their lonely fighting holes, they recited brevity codes, brainstormed scenarios, and prepared for the worst.

November 8, 2004 Fallujah, Iraq: Operation Al-Fajr (The Dawn) / Phantom Fury

At 2330 hours, the Amphibious Attack Vehicles (AAVs) moved into position on the Line of Departure (LOD). Cramped inside with 24 heads, the AAV was filled to capacity with two squads of Marines each carrying a 100-pound combat load. "Hey, can you guys see anything outside yet? I can't see shit, but it sounds like a war," X said with a smile. At 20 years old, X hailed from Baltimore. Always cheerful and generally unique, he served his unit's morale well.

"Awww damn it, I got a cramp in my leg, move over so I can stretch," Cowboy grimaced with a Tennessee twang. "Man, there ain't nowhere to move, we've been in here for hours," said Groucho, buried under the packs near the rear hatch. X exclaimed, "we need to get the fuck off of this thing before we get lit up. If this ammo starts cooking off, we'll get shot out of this can like bottle rockets!" As they moved into the attack position, everyone was holding on to whatever they could as the AAVs bounced around, negotiating the dusty, rocky terrain and sand berms surrounding the city. The diesel fumes from the exhaust crept into the back of the AmTrac, mixed with the heat, and made the Marines nauseous. Darkness filled the cabin except for a tiny bit of ambient moonlight through the top hatch.

Until this point in the war, no one from First Battalion, Third Marines (1/3) had ever experienced combat. Even the "old salt dogs" and senior enlisted men spent most of their career in a peacetime environment, with the exception of some short conflicts in Grenada, Panama, and the Persian Gulf War of the early 90's. Their minds were focused. They rehearsed the mission. They checked and rechecked their gear.

Moke was sitting on the top of the AAV with his legs over the side. He completed final checks and tinkered around with the batteries to his NVGs (Night

Vision Goggles). "You gotta be shittin' me!" he exclaimed. "I lost that little copper part that initiates the charge for the batteries. It fell off and disappeared into oblivion - fuckin' unserviceable! I never liked using these damn things anyway. Besides, you'd think we could get some of that high speed gear they issue to all the guys from 1st Mar Div, huh?"

Moke specialized in defying authority and was very outspoken. He was the kind of guy who complained about everything. Suddenly, a volley of outgoing artillery rounds began impacting targets in the city and the sky lit up with screaming streams of white phosphorous and illumination rounds. Out of the darkness, the picture of the battlefield became clear, as 50-caliber machine guns and MK-19 grenade launchers fired in succession from their mounts, revealing staggered columns of AAV's stretching for miles down the entire northern edge of Fallujah.

To improve their view, the Marines began standing up to poke their heads out of the top hatch. The awesome spectacle and effects of combined arms amazed the Marines. Sorties of air assets flew overhead and dropped their ordnance on pre-designated targets. The impressive armada included everything from F-18 Hornet fighter/bombers to F-15 Eagles, Apache and Cobra helicopters, as well as a C-130 gunship sporting the call sign "Slayer." Slayer armed itself with a Gatlin mini-gun and 105mm cannon, which produced devastating effects on the enemy, and discharged deafening and intimidating sounds when firing. Slayer circled high in the sky around the city and sounded like a giant beast vomiting after a heavy alcohol-induced sickness. The impacts shocked the atmosphere as each group of thousands of rounds penetrated millions of molecules in the air before disintegrating its target on the ground.

M1 Abram tanks moved into position and began firing their main guns combined with a consistent barrage of artillery fire from the 198mm Howitzers dug in at Camp Fallujah, only a couple miles away. This night constituted the best fireworks show any of the Marines had ever seen. They hollered and cheered for the bombardment with every blast, hoping that it was reducing the will of the enemy. Mujahadeen fighters had come from all over South West Asia, Europe, and East Africa to partake in this "Super Bowl" of battles in the Holy Land. Many of those that did not flee intended to be martyrs. With a force of about 3,000 combatants, the Mujahadeen had used the Sunni city of Fallujah as a main base of operations. The Anbar Province generally, and Fallujah specifically, represented the heart of a growing insurgency in the Sunni Triangle. Fallujah's location along the Euphrates River and close proximity to the cities of Ramadi and Bagdad provided a "fertile crescent" for insurgency.

The politics surrounding the First Battle of Fallujah (Operation Vigilant Resolve), forced American forces to withdraw from the city limits some seven months earlier. As such, the insurgency had months to fortify their strongholds without contention and prepared their defenses in order to inflict heavy casualties on the Marines. The committed insurgents dug miles of tank ditches. They buried mines and IEDs (Improvised Explosive Devices) to bog down the effort of mechanized vehicles and tanks. The IEDs were usually constructed from the guts of old artillery rounds and utilized a simple fuse, but their tactics would ultimately evolve in order to adjust to enhanced American armor. Some of the IEDs were linked together in "daisy chains" to trigger more explosions within a greater range.

The engineers launched mine-clearing line charges (MICLCs) to clear a path so the infantry units, CAAT (Combined Anti-Armor Teams), and tanks could enter the city. The engineers also brought along the indispensable D9 Bulldozer. The D9 was a massive piece of steel and machinery, capable of conquering the most formidable natural and man-made obstacles. It breached the initial defense line under fierce machine gun and rocket fire. It seemed to have almost impenetrable armor. The Marine operating the D9 remained undaunted as he worked diligently to breach the massive berm that temporarily obstructed the infantry advance.

The mission positioned First Battalion, Third Marines (1/3) on the left flank. The main effort was to attack to the West of the city near the Euphrates River. Four Marine infantry battalions (3/5, 3/1, 1/8, and 1/3) and two supporting Army Mechanized units (2/2 and 2/7) comprised the ground assault force. Following in trace was a slew of combat service support units tasked with logistics as well as medical triage and evacuations. This was a massively impressive operation, bringing all that the US military had to bear. As the left flank, 1/3's mission was to move south, punch through the lines, isolate the eastern half of the city, block any egress routes for enemy combatants, systematically engage targets, destroy any supply lines, and strategically control certain objectives (usually mosques) along the way. The initial objective was to clear a heavily fortified mosque that had been storing weapons caches, about 500 meters south of the LOD.

The months leading up to this night provided the insurgents necessary preparation time, and helped fuel something of a perfect storm, similar to the way a hurricane needs warm water and specific pressure within the atmosphere to maximize its destructive fury. As aforementioned, the fight between Marines and the Mujahadeen had been brewing for months prior, but things intensified when US forces were ordered to withdraw from the city in April of 2004. The Rules of Engagement (ROEs) were dictated by Washington politics during an election year. The same politics allowed the insurgency to fester and grow unabated, while Marines continued to die from IED's, indirect mortar and rocket fire, and snipers in the surrounding areas. Expecting heavy resistance, the Marines loaded up with enough food, water, and ammunition enough for three days, in case resupply was hindered in any way. SAPI armored plates were placed in the Marines' flak jackets for extra protection. They wore a Kevlar type material and it added another 20 pounds to their load. When a Marine asked if the SAPI plates would actually stop a bullet, the response he often received was "Well, guess you'll find out Devil."

As the bombardment continued, the Marines in the AAVs scrambled to grab all of their serialized gear and prepare to dismount when ordered. They sat in silence in the stagnant, musty air, preparing their minds for the inevitable. They listened to the static conversation on the radio. The radio made a distinctive beeping sound in between transmissions, creating an echo effect. Radio talk always has a specific verbiage and vocabulary, and sounds professional and serious. It can sound something like this: (echoing beep) "Roughneck 1... White 4, how copy? Over. Krrrrhhhhh! White 4....Roughneck 1, Lima Charlie, over." This particular example is radio jargon meaning that the guy receiving the message was able hear him "loud and clear." Learning radio language resembles learning any kind of language. Long words were replaced by acronyms. This reduced confusion and allegedly improved memory. The Marines joked about all the different acronyms that they had to remember. "Hey DD, the CO is in the CP with the BC. He's PO'd because the COG is way out in BFE in the FOB and he can't find the OOD. He needs that after action report about the CQB for the CG, so he can reassess the ROEs for the USMC". It's hilarious to hear oneself talk like that and even funnier when it makes perfect sense to the person it was being said to. After a bit of comic relief, it's back to reality.

They continued to keep their ears glued to the radio traffic, hoping for any kind of enlightening intelligence to paint a better picture of the battlefield. The Marines tried to remain calm as a rush of adrenaline constricted their muscles and flooded their veins. They all had to make some sort of peace with themselves and a higher power, if they had one. Some thought about their family, and loved ones, some guys wondered if their ladies would still love them if their dick got blown off, or if they would ever have sex again. Some guys wondered if they experienced enough in life. And some guys made resolutions if they were lucky enough to survive. Then suddenly, an explosion erupted nearby, which sounded like incoming fire.

Confusion and chatter filled the radio waves. Eventually, the back and forth chatter began making sense when reports had come in that one of the AAVs from Third Platoon, Charlie Company was hit by an IED. Moments later confirmed reports of casualties started coming through the radio. "Affirmative Spartan 6, we have at least 3 WIA's (Wounded in Action), from Spartan 3, Over."

Just moments prior to their dismount, Third Platoon Charlie's AAV pulled up near the D-9 when it took gunfire to the engine and broke down in front of the tank ditch. This set off another IED, combined with a few volleys of RPG (Rocket Propelled Grenade) attacks from the rooftops. Two squads of Marines sat in the AmTrac as the blast jolted everybody around like beans in a jar.

Those that were sitting on the right side were hit with intensive shrapnel from the blast. Several of them were saved by the thin layers of armor surrounding the AAV, but still unavoidable pieces of hot, twisted metal pierced the cabin. The Marines sitting near the point of the direct impact, absorbed most of the blast. Johns got the worst of it after losing his right arm and leg as he shielded most of the shrapnel from hitting the rest of the squad. One guy lost a finger. The concussion temporarily disoriented all of the men inside and blood splattered everywhere. Potts felt a noticeable warmth come over his body and realized that he was soaked in Johns's blood, to his right. His head was fuzzy but he could still hear their squad leader, Wolverine, calling in a mass casualty report over the radio, shouting feverishly into the mic. The Marines felt helpless as they scrambled in confusion. They were required to face the shock of their current reality.

Ironically, this was the type of thing the Marines had always trained for but never believed would actually happen. A lot of guys were on the deck of the AmTrac and covered in blood. They started to hear more small explosions outside, so they rushed out of the back of the AAV through the emergency hatch to return fire and evacuate the wounded. Suddenly, another RPG hit the other side of the AAV wounding the mounted gunner and knocking Potts down. When he regained consciousness, he could not see or hear anything. He suffered small pieces of shrapnel in his left leg and elbow, and blood leaked through his cammies. In the chaos, he got back up and began running wildly towards the enemy fire using the muzzle flashes as a beacon. He was tackled by Zeek and Duke, as they helped him back to the line where most of the Marines were returning fire in the prone position. As the Corpsman worked on Johns, Zeek oriented Potts toward the enemy, pointed his weapon down range, and screamed at him to return fire. Doc attended to Johns and applied a tourniquet to what was left of his leg and arm. All the casualties were put in a Humvee for MediVac. Potts recovered and return to the battle 5 days later. They would all eventually recover, but they never saw Johns again. He would later survive after losing both of his extremities on one side.

Meanwhile, hundreds of AmTracs are preparing to spill their load of Marines along the LOD and out into the city streets. "Alright, all you guys make your final checks on each other and get ready to dismount. We're gonna link up on the other side of the wire when we can find some cover, everybody got that?" The crew chief in the back of the AAV gave them the thumbs up with a salute, as the rear hatch slowly crept down to the deck. Simultaneously, the rest of the battalion was making the push into the city.

Everyone had their job and the assault kicked off with precise execution. The hatches dropped and scores of Marines flooded out of the AmTracs, moving to the South into the breach. Earlier that night, the rain had swept in and the tank ditch of excavated dirt turned soft and muddy. Many of the Marines were sinking knee deep in it. Their muscles had atrophied a bit and cramped up from being jammed inside the AAVs for hours during the coordinated effort. It was slow and cumbersome, adjusting to the terrain with all the weight of 100 pounds on their backs. Some of them fell to the ground in the commotion of dismounting under fire, and others fell back to help them up. They crossed through the breach site on a long, narrow patch that was dug and swept clear of mines by the engineers and the D9 Dozer. Cowboy slugged through the mud, keeping a low profile, worried that some hadgi sniper had him in his crosshairs, ready to take a shot.

The Marines expected to get hit at any moment. They jogged in a ranger file over the berm and down the other side. Every step was a potential land mine and every breath potentially their last. The squads in First Platoon became separated over the berm. Moke went back to link up. He ran through the mud puddles as he realized he was out in the open again, exposed, and feeling itchy all over. The rest of the guys made haste against the wall to the side of a building and began stacking up. Stacks are essentially a team of gunfighters lined up, one behind the other on the wall or in a column formation. They move together as a unit and cover each other from all angles - front, rear, sides and overhead. Urban environments bring a unique and complex dynamic to the battle ground. MOUT (Military Operations in Urban Terrain) is a three-dimensional battle space, to include an overhead level, street level, and a subterranean level, with a plethora of weird angles, confining spaces, and hiding places. Knowing this only increased paranoia amongst the Marines. After the preemptive fire-support had died down for the advancing infantry, a dark, black sky descended upon the city. It was eerily quiet, devoid of stars, with subtle gusts of a cool breeze, and sprinkling rain. It seemed like everything was in slow motion. Nerves were hypersensitive. The Marines utilized a lot of deep breaths to control their adrenaline.

Moke linked up with the rest of the squad and they ran back to the rally point. Their orders were to support Bravo Section from 2nd Tanks out of Camp Lejeune, N.C. They all moved up along the wall. Weed peeked around the corner down the dark, narrow street. Weighing "a buck fifty," he had a slender silhouette, spittin' a dip with a calm, country swagger. The Assault Section set up the SMAW (Shoulder-Launch, Multi-Purpose, Attack Weapon), and fired a rocket down the street blowing up a parked car. Everything was treated as a potential IED. They had to quickly learn to distinguish the difference between a potential threat and merely an inanimate object, like garbage. They were happy to see the M1 Abram tanks pull up and move into position. They had special thermal sights within the tank's technology to get good eyes on a target in complete darkness. As it began creeping down the street, the squads followed in trace.

The surrounding buildings were stacked two to three levels up, with high walls and iron gates. Some of the houses were beautifully constructed mansions with fertilized green grass, while surrounded by dust and dirt. It was a place so wanting of flora to ever suggest that such a beautiful lawn of grass would be naturally indigenous to the region. However, history refers to this land of antiquity as the once lush greenery of the "Garden of Eden" and "Fertile Crescent." Armies have battled on the same grounds for centuries in the hopes of acquiring its abundant resources and trade routes. For millennia, it was a strategic location intersecting the Silk and Spice Roads that connected Asia and Europe. The demand for spices and trading goods in this modern era, have been replaced by the need for oil. Petroleum is the very blood of a mechanized superpower.

The squads organized and staggered themselves into columns to allow for some dispersion in case of an ambush. Groucho, the point man, took a knee as he noticed a silver, metallic liquid, balling up in the sand. He had some of it on his cammies and he brushed it off as it burned a small hole into his sleeve. "Hey guys! Heads up, there is "Willie Pete" (White Phosphorous) everywhere and that shit is still burnin", he said in amazement. It littered the streets in globs, the residue of exploded ordinance from artillery rounds dropped to prepare for the attack of US forces. "Clank, clank, clank," the tank tracks rumbled onto the loose asphalt. Their call sign was aptly "Blitzkrieg." As the Abrams crept along, the squad walked on the flanks covering the angles and overhead. The tank's rear exhaust emitted intense heat with the roaring sound of a jet engine. However, things still seemed silent enough to hear a pin drop. First Platoon constituted only one of several units operating adjacent to one another, each tasked with a specific area of operation (AO). They moved in line from North to South like a tsunami. As they bounded from house to house, the "crack, crack" of AK-47 fire whizzed by. The AK had a distinctive sound when it was fired at them, as opposed to it being fired away from them, like snapping dry branches off a tree. Everyone dropped to the deck and fired back into the upper levels of the surrounding buildings. "Contact right!" they all yelled. Shooter dropped on his back with a thump and emptied a magazine into the building. It then occurred to him how much ammunition and explosives were strapped to him. Gunfire erupted from all sides and it was difficult to tell where it was coming from.

The whole platoon emptied a magazine or SAW drum, reloaded, and racked the bolt. The first fire engagement jitters were alleviated. Fried Rice yelled out for a Corpsman. Doc C ran over to him and cut open his bloody sleeve. "Ah, it's just a scratch man," said Doc C, as he applied pressure with a bandage to stop the bleeding. Moke ran over and ducked behind the cover of the tank to talk with the crew inside of the tank on the "grunt phone". "Blitzkrieg...Spartan 1. Roger Spartan 1, send it. "Yeah we got some initial contact from the right flank from the second deck of those houses. Can you scan your thermals up there and see a sniper?" The tank turned it's turret up 45 degrees and to the right. He fired some rounds from the .50 cal machine gun mount. Blitzkrieg confirmed he shot at a heated silhouette lying on the second deck. "Spartan 1, I pumped a few rounds in there and he's not moving." Moke responded, "Roger that...tango Blitzkrieg...Spartan 1 out." He ran back to the squad and crouched near a burned out car.

Seconds were like minutes and minutes like hours. The Marines were jumpy and anxious about what dawn would bring. They were all crouched along the wall facing inboard and overhead. Point and tail-end-charlie covered the avenues of approach up and down the street. Everyone was fighting the urge to succumb to the intense exhaustion that consumed their bodies. After the adrenaline had peeled away, they were left to retrieve their inner core. It was pre-dawn and the sun was beginning to break the seal of darkness that blanketed the sky. They had to get off the street and enter a house to re-group. They busted the gate of a two story corner house with a balcony, which was perfect. A late 80's model Mercedes sat in the driveway. Only because they had to stay in this particular house for a while, did everyone repel the urge to throw an incendiary grenade on the motor block and melt it into scrap metal. They cleared the house and set up a temporary observation post on the roof to get a clear view of the mosque, their first objective. Everyone took turns catching a wink, eating some chow, and making adjustments to gear. It was dark as hell. It was cloudy and the moon was obscured, blocking the ambient light, rendering the NVGs almost worthless. Second and Third Platoons of Charlie Company had been fighting sporadically through the night on the adjacent streets. There were between 15-30 insurgents defending the mosque, and it became a legitimate target the minute they began firing from it. On the adjacent street to the West, Nike and Lifer had their squads positioned on rooftops, overlooking an open field where the enemy was pinned down in the mosque. Pandemonium ensued, as a barrage of AT-4 rockets and grenade launchers erupted. RPG's were fired in return from enemy emplacements, whizzing overhead, as the Marines saturated the area with hot metal.

Some of the leaders from Third Platoon concerned themselves with insurgents moving to flank them from the rear. Suddenly, a fire team of about six enemy fighters made a run during a brief pause in firing. SAW (Squad Automatic Weapon) gunners from Lifer's squad opened up and cut them down immediately in their tracks. Their bodies were riddled and motionless. They were making a desperate attempt to move to fall back position. Casper watched them lying there, trying to judge the distance between his guys and the dead insurgents in the field.

At dawn, the sun poked over the horizon, and the gunfight resumed with intensity. The tank escort left its position to engage the plentiful targets that poured out of the mosque. Moke had crashed for about an hour of intense slumber, sitting up with his head back and mouth open. It was an otherwise perfect scenario for some fun, sexual innuendos at his expense. He woke up with a snort and blurry red eyes, as a few guys laughed at his vulnerability. "What?" he said, looking bamboozled. More gunfire resumed as machine guns moved at the cyclic rate. Orders were passed on the radio from higher "to move out, take the ground, and engage the enemy." Everyone scrambled to get their gear on, picking up loads of ammo and rockets. They all assembled in the doorway out to the courtyard. Wildo looked around real quick, counting heads. "Alright Gents, this is what we've been waiting for. We're about to walk into the fight of our lives!" They poured out into the street and assembled into staggered columns, bounding, and covering in textbook fashion. The effects of the earlier bombardments on the battlefield were evident.

They bobbed and weaved through the rubble, and down the streets, covering and firing to protect their movement. The mosque was on fire, and bodies littered the ground. It was some glorified destruction from Third Platoon. Some of the dead were suspended from rooftops and window sills, like the stunts you see in the movies. As the Marines ran passed them, the grim reality was apparent to everyone that this wasn't a game or a training evolution. The dead wore ammunition vests, old style camouflage gear, and tennis shoes. Wildo noticed the shoes specifically, because they were brand-new and gleaming white. It was like the dead guy had just taken them out of the box the night before. One corpse lied on his back staring to the sky as if in complete anticipation of heaven, as blood trickled dry from the hole in his head. He looked plastic with rigor mortis. He wasn't a threat anymore, and they spit on him as they ran by. "Die you fuckin' Muj!" It was hardcore, but they didn't have time to process their primal instincts....just go, kill, and win!

They covered a distance of 1500 meters in about 10 minutes to their second objective, a series of half constructed buildings next to another mosque. It became known as the "Dash, Down Charles" in reference to the brevity name that was given for that particular street. They covered the ground quickly, amid enemy sniper and machine gun fire. The enemy began to hastily displace back to alternative defensive positions deeper into the city. They knew they couldn't hold off the advancing grunts, but only hope to delay for as long as possible and inflict as many casualties as they could. The Marines were expending a seemingly endless supply of ammunition, 40 mm grenades, and AT-4 rockets. They were distracted from the fact that bullets were flying all around them, and some just ignored the shrapnel bouncing through their flesh. After the squads were getting bunched up, Moke began barking orders to disperse, and seek cover when JD passed out and fell to the ground. They thought he'd been hit, but instead he was suffering from heat exhaustion – a constant and very real threat. They were in an open area at an intersection and it was a bad place to be. "You gotta be shitting me! You're gonna lie down as a heat case in the middle of a fuckin' firefight, get the fuck up! You're gonna take three guys out of the fight to carry your fuckin' ass...get the fuck up. We gotta make it across the street." JD was a stocky guy. They were each weighed down with 100 pounds of gear combined with the massive amount of sweat that evaporated into their cammies. None of them had the strength to throw over three hundred pounds over their back and fireman's carry JD to the objective.

All of sudden Weed comes running up with an AT-4 and quickly yells out "back-blast area all secure"...BOOM! He fired it inches from Cowboy's ear, as he immediately went deaf on his left side. Weed shot the rocket through a window across the street from where they were taking some fire, and blew out the inside room. Shards of glass and twisted metal, shot from out of the building. "What the fuck?" Cowboy grabbed his head and looked over at Weed, bewildered. He couldn't hear anything, so he attempted to read his lips. "I got that motherfucker...did you see that!?" No, but I heard it so much I'm deaf you asshole!" The deafening subsided to ringing, and eventually, the ringing became the muffled sound of a spoken word. JD gathered himself enough to be carried with help under his own power. They all linked up under a shanty roof-covered bazaar on the corner of the street. Looking down to the West, they noticed three Mujahadeen fighters running across the street in black pajamas and carrying an RPK (Soviet medium machine gun) and some AK-47's. They were like lightning bolts. After a quick glimpse, they were gone. A few of the Marines saw them, fired at them, and got all riled up for a chase, only to be pulled back by the "Company Guns," the Company Gunnery Sergeant. It was an affectionate term for the second highest enlisted rank within a company of Marines. "Sandman" had a commanding presence and street credit, with a nonchalant, but hard ass attitude. He was a Marine from the Old Corps. With a slurred Philly accent he said, "Get the fuck back here Devil Dawgs, what the fuck you think you gonna do...win the war in a day?"

After regrouping under the Bazaar, the squads displaced around the surrounding buildings near their objective, a mosque, perpendicular to a large, open field. They all huddled down on a berm while coordinating with higher command to clear the objective, establish a foothold, and gain intelligence (intel). The M1 tank slowly crept around the corner of the street, when an insurgent fired an RPG from a window. The RPG disabled the tank's engine from behind as internal fluids began spraying out. It was too tight of a spot to fire back with the tank's main gun, so the attackers were met with a heavy barrage of M240 machine gun fire and M203, launched, grenades. Everyone had their head down, shielding their faces from all the flying rocks and debris. After the smoke cleared, they poked up their heads with a few hoots and hollers, and echoed a resilient "fuck you!", and the enemy was silenced. The "word" came down from Spartan 6, a.k.a. Captain Quiet (call sign for the Company Commander) on the platoon's next move. Bean Stalk relayed the incoming radio transmission to the rest of the guys. "Hey... 6 said this is our Limit of Advance (LOA) for now, he wants us to clear these buildings and set up an OP (Observation Post). Then, we have to send out a patrol into that scrap yard across the street, neutralize any potential threats, and secure that mosque." Bean Stalk possessed a gift for talking on the radio. The guys always felt better knowing he was the liaison of communication.

The squads picked up and filed off into clearing the first and second levels of the structure. It was half-constructed with brick and plaster containing several rooms without windows. It wasn't exactly a comfortable home, but it was in a good position from which to resupply and execute patrols. Directly across the main street was the mosque, Objective B. It was necessary to capture many of the mosques in the city so they could not be used as protected havens for the insurgents to wage a fight. Naturally for Muslims, the mosque is a place where they feel the most empowered by their God, and certainly a prophetic symbol around which to mount a fierce defense. Under the ROE's, the mosques were not to be destroyed or defaced in any way, provided that they were not used as shooting positions, which was often the case. So rather than offer that type of sanctuary to the enemy, American forces strategically controlled these objectives to save them from being demolished. This particular mosque was empty with a large rug furnishing the floor. It was a culture shock of religion, customs, and smells. Some of the men were surprised to see green grass within the walled compound.

A check around the premises revealed that there had been recent activity there. The tanks were engaging sporadic targets in the scrap yard. Deuce watched in amazement from a crouched position as an insurgent ran across the open area between two cars. The COAX machine guns from the M1 were relentless at eliminating short range-moving targets, riddling the car's cheap metal with holes. The guns literally chopped him into pieces with the merciless barrage of fire. It was bloody, gruesome, and raw, as pieces of his screaming flesh were splattered over the ground. Deuce had been recently reincarnated from his boyhood insecurities since the night before. A young, small town kid, he grew up to be a man, overnight. No longer unsure and naïve, his eyes would lay testament to his own rebirth.

Upon further investigation, the Marines noticed a small suspicious car parked at the corner of the wall. Inside it, the Marines found weapons, explosives, and most notably, an American-made M249 SAW, light machine gun. The first thought that ran through their minds was how they obtained this weapon, and why did they leave it here? Was it taken from a dead Marine, or is it a booby trap? The car was full of garbage and wiring, so they made a quick sweep for possible intel and called in the demo guys to blow it in place. Napoleon, the leader of the assault section, loved to be called to rig up explosives. It was his passion and he was good at it. "Hey, we need some punch to dispatch this problem. I don't want to use all the C4 we got. Bring up those Bangalore torpedoes." Those types of explosives were originally used to breach obstacles, but since they were already embedded in the city, toting them around was becoming dead weight at 30 pounds per pipe. He assembled the three sections and spliced them together. Then, he slid it under the car after he popped the blasting cap and ignited the fuse. The demolition team was escorted by a fire team for security, as they positioned themselves to cover the scrap yard and down the avenues of approach. Seconds later, Napoleon came running around the corner with his guys in trace, "fire in the hole!" he shouted. They all dashed across the street and around the corner of a wall, with a few seconds to spare and plugged their ears to equalize the pressure of the blast. "Boom!" The concussion passed through their bodies like an invisible shockwave, as fire, smoke, and metal shot into the air, completely obliterating the IED threat and the wall on the side of the mosque. It was a good thing because it cleared out any obstruction for observing targets from the platoon's objective. They all laughed and looked at each other after the smoke cleared. Nothing of the car remained. It became a vacant parking spot. "There's no such thing as overkill! Yeah, yeah, yeah! The scrap yard still needed to be dissected further before it could be considered "secure".

They had their work cut out for them in the days ahead, but for now, the sun was setting over the horizon as the dark silhouette of minarets dominated the city skyline. They all began filtering into the building and staking a claim to specific spots on the floor where they would sleep that night. For a moment they were temporarily disengaged from the battle outside, to share a smoke and a joke. Everything to that point had transpired so fast. There wasn't enough time to really digest what was going on. They still had to make a "fire watch" roster, and someone would inevitably get fucked in that deal. They took some time to throw down some chow in their bellies, dust off their weapons, or maybe jot down some quick words. But it was just the beginning. They were not yet numb to adrenaline or death. They were full of excitement; a healthy fear, and a free exuberance that is not often known in a man's life. War was their business now, programmed with enough cognitive reception to temper an instinctively barbaric inclination to lay waste to all things living. It was an amazing time to be chewing sand with the Marines of Fallujah.

Chapter 2
Back to the Future

Eight months earlier, the Lava Dawgs (the nickname earned by Battalion 1/3 because of the volcanic, island terrain of Hawaii) were based in garrison at Kaneohe Bay, Marine Corps Base Hawaii (MCBH). K-Bay represented an oasis of sun and surf in the vastness of the Pacific Ocean. For many, it was the top pick on the duty station "wish list," especially for those skating through the end of their career to retirement. During the deployment build up, the battalion needed to increase it numbers in the rifle companies. There was a lot of confusion and administrative changes, as they shifted Marines around from different companies and assigned new roles. This created a uniquely contentious situation.

The Iraq War was ramping up and replacements were needed to fill the void in 3rd Marine Regiment, on the island. The generals and all their infinite wisdom decided to drop a select number of guys from 3rd Battalion into 1st Battalion, who were mostly senior in time and grade. They all had already completed two overseas deployments, which at that time was the usual at a three-year duty station. However, in 2003 the deployment cycle was altered when the battalion was split up, and contingents were deployed to Bahrain and the Philippines. This disrupted the normal deployment schedule, and required changes in manpower. Some of the guys who were considered junior to the senior guys from 3rd Battalion had already been involved in supporting special operations against guerrillas in Zamboanga. Obvious problems began to stoke up when some guys were demoted and others promoted. Marines are fiercely loyal to those whom they serve and experience earns respect. Any "outsiders" were suspect from the beginning. The new drops were also well inclined to represent who they are, and where they had been, so it became a bona fide pissing contest.

The Battalion Commander, Mad Mike was incessant on getting the Lava Dawgs into a real world mission. It was the ultimate chess game in the officer world. He would have to optimize his strategy and grease the skids to move the battalion along and position themselves perfectly. Every day for months, they had no clue of their destiny, but they trained and worked out the kinks, the way every deployment cycle evolves. The grunts spent much of their working days preparing for the next "pump" with the 31st MEU from Okinawa, which was scheduled for that July. The only problem was that the battalion had failed considerably during the qualification exercises and they had to meet a certain criteria during the "work up" phase to be viable for the Marine Expeditionary Unit's mission. The usual rumors were flying around about what the future might hold, but it was best not to speculate. Either way, it would probably suck.

When the Marines were not training in the field, they took advantage of any raucously, inebriated, leisure time they could get. Every weekend, they left a trail of carousal in their wake stretching from K-Bay to Waikiki. "Liberty" was a time best suited for the moment and they indulged in their capacity for festive debauchery. However, they stood out as Marines and if they did something stupid, civilians knew who to blame. It was impossible to hide the haircut. It was a dead giveaway - forget about being anonymous. The shorter the hair, the more likely they were identifiable. Their tradition directly correlates with what happens next...drinking and fighting. That adversely affected any chances of finding a girl for the night, which was always the end game. Every week, they were shaved skin tight around the ears. Many of those that rated it, tried to keep a "low-regs" profile (referring to a low regulation haircut) and stretched the rules for the hair on top (3 inches). They were the disgruntled members of the Corps, considered "salty." One had to earn longer hair and mustaches with "time in service." This was among several of the unwritten rules.

These grunts regularly wandered around the likes of Lewers Street in Downtown Waikiki, and frequented places like Kelly O'Neils, Moose's, Irish Rose, Red Lion, and Tropics that were synonymous with hard charging, drinking extravaganzas. Waves of Marines blew their paychecks from Friday to Sunday on the first weekend of the 1st and the 15th of each month. They flooded the joint with round after round of Jager Bombs and Irish Car Bombs. The bars didn't close until 4 am and there was a constant flow of tourists from the mainland to entertain the relentless, weekend fuck-fests. It would be an even better story to tell their buddies on a field op, if she admitted to having a boyfriend back home, but she still fucked him anyway. Plunder and pillage with epic enthusiasm. The raunchy reality of the cycle was priceless. They absorbed their toxic limits, desperately subscribing to subdue the anxiety that perpetuates anticipation. It was a fast life maximized by a deeply-ingrained, barbarous mentality.

April 2004 Kahuku Training Area, Oahu, Hawaii

"Why the fuck are we patrolling in the jungle, with blank rounds, when there's a war going on in the desert," exclaimed Soup Can. The senior guys in the company always had a candid way of looking at things. They would often rally up during some down time to discuss their caustic reality, around a session of packing a fat wad of tobacco in their lips, and playing "spit on the Gatorade cap." Many of them were going on their third deployment, and they were a little bitter about it. It was a numbers game, early on in the war before retention exploded due to the economy. Many of them had plans to skate the next year, and maybe get a sweet TAD (Temporary Assigned Duty) like working at the pool or the satellite gym on base. With less than a year left on their enlistments, they could only imagine the misery that would shortly ensue. Uncle Sam would extract every penny from them. They were trained for jungle warfare. The last time their unit had seen any real combat was Vietnam, with the exception of an 8 month, extended field op in Saudi Arabia during Operation Desert Shield.

They wanted a chance to get in the shit, but disillusionment ran rampant among the ranks as the war in Iraq intensified and the entire 3rd Marine Division remained excluded. As far as they knew, they were just in it for another ride on the "Iron Coffin," sailing Gator Squares in the middle of the Pacific with the Thirty Worst MEU (31st Marine Expeditionary Unit), a continuously, afloat, amphibious readied force able to answer a call in days from anywhere within its AO. It still remained the indigenous mission of the Marine Corps, but at that time the fight was in Iraq, and it was the only place to be. "Hey, who's got a cell phone? Let's order a pizza," said Soup Can. They all started to chuckle. "We'll organize a recon patrol to the road for pick-up...hey Smiley, you still got that flask of Jack?" "Yup", he said, with a grin. They called him Smiley because he didn't smile much unless he was drunk or thinking about getting drunk. It wasn't so much a job, as it was a primitive camping adventure with friends.

The Kahuku's were infamous for rain and misery. The Marines had been living in the mountains and training there for weeks, just running around the woods, looking to capture a boot from the other platoons and tie him up as a hostage. Occasionally they would ride around in helicopters to practice raids and civilian evacuations. The recent months of their deployment build-up pretty much consisted of patrolling, aimlessly, with blank rounds in their weapons, while scarcely funded for better training because budget priorities went to the battalions that were actually deployed to combat. In some cases, the new "boot" Marines had to use sticks to simulate a rifle because they had not yet been issued one. It was absurd in many ways. But considering they had no idea they would end up fighting for their lives against an insurgency in an urban, desert environment, they wasted precious time playing hide and seek in the jungle with sticks and BFA's (Blank Firing Attachment). The senior Marines knew of the slight possibility they could go to Iraq, but the scuttlebutt could never be confirmed until they actually knew it. It was just a big mind fuck of "what if" and "hurry up and wait." The small-unit leaders still accepted that it was their responsibility to ensure the Marines were prepared for that possibility, and it was frustrating to think they were jerking off on a mountain in Hawaii, without the tools to train.

"You're preaching to the fuckin' choir, Soup Can!! Fuck this shit man. I'm getting a pizza...who's got cash," said Zob. They thrived off rebellious tom foolery. It was improvisation at its best. Making an uneventful training evolution into a real mission that had a great purpose. They would need to employ their skills to successfully evade detection and complete the mission without any trace of the evidence. They all put their money together, enough for two large pizzas, two slices for each man. Zob called Domino's with one bar left on his cell phone. "Ah, yes ma'am, what kind of specials do you have? Ah-uh, and do you have banana peppers?" He talked for a few minutes, giving them the specifics of their order. Moments later he came walking around a tree. "Hey, they said it would be about 45 minutes, I told him we'd meet him on the road at Charlie Gate, across from Turtle Bay." They all made silent cheer and rubbed their hands together with salivating tongues. They anticipated the mission's success and the thought of the look on the pizza guy's face when they jumped out of the trees, dirty with camouflage, made it even more mischievous. They set off down the hill, through the dense foliage, maintaining light and noise discipline. It was imperative that they were not detected by other patrolling squads in the area or a possible ambush that would compromise their hunger for the delectable dough and cheese.

After about 30 minutes, they reached the last checkpoint near the road. All that was left to do was lay outboard in a circle and remain silent and still. Minutes passed and a slight, steady drizzle fell just enough to soak their cammies (camouflage uniform) for the night. Soup was looking down the long, narrow, single lane highway when he spotted the Domino's sign on top of a Toyota Civic. He was about to run into the street and flag him down when Moke grabbed his arm. "Gimme your fuckin' weapon...are you crazy man? You want that guy shittin' his pants all over our pizza', he chuckled. "Oh yeah, I'm fuckin' starving", said Soup. The guy stopped in front of the walled entrance. He was startled and shocked as Soup Can approached him with his hands up, laughing. "Hey man, it's cool...I just want the pizza, I have money." They all watched from the tree line as the entertaining spectacle transpired. "Whoa bra, I neva knew one Army guy ordered dis, where you came from?" "Haaaa, up in those mountains and we're Marines bra," said Soup. "Whoa...you guys crazy, huh? Haaa, OK take em' bra, enjoy da "grinds," look like you guys been eating dirt for da pass week," he said. "Mahalo," replied Soup Can as he ran back into the tree line.

They ripped open the boxes and devoured their allotted two pieces per man within a few bites like wild dogs. Smiley pulled out the flask and they passed it around for a swig. They celebrated their accomplishment. After burying the cardboard evidence, they made haste down the dirt road leading back up into the mountains. All of a sudden headlights shined from the bottom of the hill. "Oh shit, disappear!!" Moke ran off the road, temporarily blinded by the headlights, obscuring his natural night vision. He ran straight into a barbed-wire fence, flipped over upside down, and was hung up by his gear. He surrendered himself to any movement, as the patrolling Humvee slowly passed. Laughing and bleeding from puncture holes in his skin, Moke began to yell for the guys to cut him loose, his cammies were ripped near his ass, and he would have to wear them for a few more days. "Damn, I didn't pack a sewing kit or a second set of clothes!"

The Marines spent Monday through Friday in the field. After the week was over, they guys would be all psyched up, riding the bus back to K-Bay through the North Shore, best known for big-wave surfing and the Banzai Pipeline. Sometimes, the budget allowed transport via "birds" and they would ride CH-53 helicopters back to the flight line of Kaneohe, which dramatically expedited the transition to "Liberty Call". They would all stack up in the armory, in filthy fatigues and muddy boots, frantically cleaning their weapons so they could turn them in, and get cut loose. "Hey, I haven't shit in a week. What's the government not telling us about what they put in those MREs? I need a double cheese, please, and I'll be singing "Praise Jesus" on my porcelain throne! I buy, you fly," said a Marine with an exaggerated laugh. "Fly boot, fly", as he handed a mandatory volunteer a 20 dollar bill. "Get 13 of them, enough for the squad." It was a glorious time for them.

The weekend was full of possibilities, and they were wild animals, released into society. "Ey yo, Zeek....we hittin' the Ki's tonight, Kelly's and Mooses? Pre-game at Tropics, and then you know the Bat Mobile is in full effect," referring to a Nissan 240SX, slightly modified from its original appearance to invoke "creep mode." Zeek just gave him a nod, and replied, "Yo dawg, I got the torch. I'm gonna be lightin' bitches up, Yeah, yeah, yeah!" The start of those conversations would be followed up with a sinister laugh and the cognitive zeal of one's own sexual prowess. It was back to the endless pursuit of a one night stand. They didn't have time to feel anything for the unbridled slew of females. If on the off chance, they did catch feelings, deploying halfway across the world would sabotage it in a few months.

Those months passed by and before they knew it, they were being pricked with the small pox vaccine en route to Okinawa to link up with the 31st MEU. For the guys who had one, they were kissing their wives goodbye. For the married Marines, deployments presented an entirely different challenge. Single life was a break from responsibilities and grunts already had enough of that in their day job. They needed an outlet and the guys who were "wifed up" were usually too young to recognize such a timely experience. The weight of that paper placed a lot of stress on the couple and never afforded them an excuse for the occasional extramarital, lovers tryst. They were forced to abstain from the natural inclination of a grunt's vigorous enthusiasm for Liberty. Instead they were relegated to hang out with other married guys and take pictures at touristy places. Breaking the marriage sacrament often led to a Courts Martial and possible discharge. And of course, they already had about a hundred pairs of eyes watching them, ready to rat out the cheaters. Semper Fidelis. The whole marriage idea often proved to be a double-edged sword for young Marines, despite the apparent financial benefits. It's a discipline that reveals unreciprocated sacrifice. While Marines are deployed overseas, they presume that their wives or girlfriends are patiently and monogamously waiting for them to return home.

The Marines often joked about the legend of Jodie, however, a Marine's ego usually gets in the way of believing that it could actually happen to him. Is she really out riding Jodie for a late night session, or is it just the same old scuttlebutt? If a boot infantryman became married during his first enlistment, he immensely complicated his life. Many of these "post-teens" ignore the transition to adulthood. They are often too young to understand the ramifications of matrimony, and do not usually possess the maturity to accept the kind of sacrifice their marriage will demand. Long deployments take a toll on family cohesion. She gets bored and lonely, and realizes she missed out on youthful opportunities. A standard practice of some is getting pregnant before a deployment to keep her occupied. Otherwise, she has full access to his bank account and knows he gets paid on the 1st and the 15th. With no responsibility, she's got a seven month paid vacation courtesy of the US Government. Then she's a regular at the E-Club and everyone knows her first name. She ignores the full implications of her husband's service, because in the event he dies, her name is on the SGLI life insurance policy (worth $400,000) that he signed to her before he shipped out to combat. It's not rocket science to figure out why these young kids get married to lance corporals and PFCs, straight out of high school. The government will facilitate this perpetual affair, essentially, with a blank check. They make double the money as a single Marine for doing the same job, a house on base with free utilities, 100% medical for everyone, and basically free of any real world responsibilities.

Many Marines also arrange contract marriages with women they will never see or hardly know from back home just to get the extra pay and "separation" benefits for living in a different state. For young girls straight out of high school, it's an easy scam to upgrade from living in their parent's house in Podunk, USA to exotic duty stations around the world. And moreover, the system sanctions a license to procreate. Apparently, the military has a method to this madness. Early into war, there are a lot of logistical and administrative changes that occur. The Corps needs Marines with dependents to maintain its annual retention rate. The logic being, that you will dedicate your life to the government, have too many kids, and accrue too much debt to ever consider leaving the Marines. When they do the math, it makes more sense to keep them as long as they have use for them, especially considering they have invested tens of thousands of dollars to train, feed, and house them. The government accepts this financial burden because they need to keep them "dependent"...on the Corps first and the family second. Usually a new marriage doesn't outlast a first deployment.

Vice versa, the system can still just "phase them out" whenever appropriate to "trim the fat." It's all about numbers. Worrying about a wife and kids is definitely a conflict of interest in a combat zone, especially as a grunt. That kind of thing will get somebody killed in addition to the thousand other ways. However, there is always "that guy." The guy who is so enamored by his young, 20 year old vixen, college girlfriend- type, he signed her as Power of Attorney, to keep his Jeep while he went off to war. Next thing he knows, three months into the deployment, he receives some mail. It was postage stamped with the county seal of Hawaii, dated two months prior. The letter was a notice of accruing an outstanding balance at the car impound in Honolulu. His supposed girlfriend was arrested for DUI while joy riding around Waikiki, in his jeep, with another guy. It's a painful kick in the balls to be 10,000 miles away from home, with 6 months left in country, and have to listen to his buddies cracking that same joke, who "told him so".

August 2004, USS Essex LHD-2, somewhere in the Indian Ocean.

(Whistle blowing over the ship's intercom) "Reveille...Reveille! Get up, get up Charlie Corps! We've got morning clean up in the head this week," said the duty NCO. "Hey, wake up, SSGT needs some bodies from your squad for the working party." "Ahhhh! What the fuck Turbo? I was just dreaming about bangin' this hot filipino chick. You fucked up my happy ending; look I pitched a tent just for you." He picked his head off the pillow and slid onto his side, holding his protruding erection from underneath the poncho liner. "Wow...you love me that much, huh"? , said

Turbo. "Put that little thing away". He crawled out of the coffin rack (a reference to narrow bunk beds on a Navy ship) and hit his head on the rack above. Half awake, his feet hit the floor. "Team leaders...need one from each of you for a working party. Report to the duty-NCO for morning clean-up in the head." The squad leader hated having to give up a name and fuck up some guy's breakfast, but no one was immune to forced penetration in the continuous ass-raping of "Operation Green Weenie." "If all you dirt bags would just clean as you go, it wouldn't be such a fuckin' sty in there," he shouted.

It had been two weeks since they left Okinawa for an undisclosed mission, in an undisclosed location, under a classified status. For many of the senior Marines, it was their second time on the ship. There wasn't much to do except eat, sleep, read, work out, and get figuratively butt-fucked at the company's discretion. The job for the Marines doesn't really begin until they disembark the ship. While on board, there is plenty of time to play "fuck-fuck games," an affectionate term used to describe business as usual. They lived in cramped quarters with racks stacked four high, and a walkway the width of a man's shoulders for eight Marines and their gear. The entire berthing space was about the equivalent size of a two-car garage for 80 men. When they would bend over to put on their pants and lace up their boots, there was a good chance they'd be staring at another guy's ass. There was no privacy and space was a luxury that only the officers enjoyed in the top decks. There were restrictions on tobacco use, no alcohol, and virtual celibacy, unless it was within your pay grade, of course. It was the redundancy of things - hygiene, uniform appearance, boredom and the usual hour-long wait in a line stretching nearly the entire length of the ship for some hot chow (food). It usually included a daily dose of processed eggs, a burnt piece of bacon, and a soft oily hash brown. The alternative was skipping the line, and filling up on an unlimited supply of cereal, provided the cooler in the galley still had fresh milk.

The Marines were trained as a helicopter insertion company, executing a wide range of missions, including humanitarian support. Scuttlebutt was filtering down that the higher-ups were formulating a plan to do an amphibious landing in Kuwait, and conduct two weeks of training exercises and then return to the ship. It was met with staunch criticism and complaints by all the guys in the ship's berthing, lying stacked on one another in the gear locker atop a mound of sea bags. "Why would they off-load all that gear for a two week field op? That's bullshit, makes no sense why don't they just let us go in already and fuck some shit up," ranted Sloth. "Nah man, Mad Mike has something up his sleeve. I heard he was trying to get the battalion geared up for Fallujah. They're planning a big operation to take back the city," said Groucho. "Where did you hear that from," asked Cowboy. "Someone's wife said she heard it from CNN?" They all laughed with a shrug, "yeah whatever."

Unbeknownst to the Marines, Mad Mike had indeed politicized his way into Kuwait. The ships were running out of food and supplies to support the Marines on board. They would need to off-load on land, and figure out a place to stage themselves for the next move. After a month at sea, they started issuing sets of desert fatigues to all the Marines, however the mission was not yet confirmed. Early in September, orders began to trickle down from the top in preparation for a landing in Kuwait. Gear lists, inspections, and more games. Many of them ignored the optional cold weather gear, considering it was still a 100 plus degrees outside. They wouldn't be there that long, and besides, how cold could it get in the desert?

September 2004 Persian Gulf / Kuwait

The Marines filed off from the lines into stacks of 24 men, as the CH-53 Sea Stallion's propeller snapped and whipped up the air. The ramps were down and the crew chiefs gave the signal to embark the "birds." They had practiced it a hundred times, but for them, this mission would give new meaning to the term "expeditionary." Loaded down with a hundred pounds of gear, everything they would need for the weeks ahead. A fresh shot of adrenaline pumped through their veins, as the coordinated chaos enveloped the ship's flight deck. One by one they were counted with a swift pat on the shoulder. The ramp went up and moments later, weightlessness and a view of blue as the ship shrunk in size until it was tiny compared to the vast surrounding sea. The heat was intense, and not even the breeze flowing through the helicopter doors was enough to hold back the dripping sweat on their faces. The screaming engine perforated their ear drums. It would be almost an hour flight until their boots would hit the sand. However, the guys from Charlie were grateful to be helo-borne. Charlie would already be first on deck, with claims to a cot, and a chow hall taste test. They spent the next month working out the kinks within small unit scenarios and rehearsed convoy operations to combat the growing threat of IEDs. They were still not privy to the specifics, but the word spread that their mission was going to be something big. One thing was evident - it wasn't going to be a two-week training evolution in Kuwait.

The battalion was headed North, and that only meant one thing, Iraq. Everyone scrambled to get as much of the luxury items, usually reserved for garrison life, as possible. PX runs, chow hall food, showers, flush toilets, air conditioning, phone calls home, and the Internet were primary examples. Maybe a guy was lucky enough to scoop up some "Army punani" in a dark, vacant tent and pass on the cognitive images to his buddy to save for a late night jerk session. Either way, their war seemed imminent and many of them had already written their "blood letter" (last letter home to family before dying). Half of the battalion was divided into a convoy force, while the remaining half would be inserted from helicopters. It would take the convoy three days to go three hundred miles. They prepared the "new" Humvee, gun trucks, complete with 3 inch, thick armor doors and bullet proof glass. A welcomed addition to the modified, older version, which was hastily fitted with iron plating, welded to the doors from scrap metal. Indicative of the general misallocation of military resources, the most heavily armored and best equipped vehicles were acquisitioned to only the most privileged among the ranks, instead of those actually spearheading the fight. These notions, coupled with a plethora of other imbalances, served as a grim reality of their general expendability. However, nothing could be more glorious than to die in the defense of America's divine jurisdiction to employ a ceaseless, offense.

October 2004 - Convoy into Iraq

"Load and Lock".... an anonymous transmission squawked across the airwaves. They all racked their bolts to the rear, chambering a round into their weapons, as they made exit outside the wire. It was good-bye to Kuwait, knowing that they were leaving the best chance of any relative safety that they were going to see from then on. It was a sobering thought. All the training, complaining, and preparation had led them to this point. The landscape at the border turned into barbed-wire, sand berms, and old blown out, Soviet made, Iraqi tank emplacements left where they had died and rusted. A slow rolling fog blanketed the area, as children lined the road. Their faces were revealed by the early morning mist. They came running out from dilapidated, mud covered shacks. Drapes of tattered cloth covered the holes dug out for windows. The children were barefoot, with beautifully dirty faces, devoid of smiles. Their raggedy clothes hung from their starving bodies. It was a somber sight to see for such green eyes. The convoy stretched out for miles with hundreds of vehicles, one of the largest sea borne elements to deploy in force.

The drivers were trained to maintain at least a 100-meter cushion between each vehicle to minimize the potential impact of IED's along the way. IEDs were the big killer at that moment. They didn't worry so much about getting shot. It was getting blown to oblivion and having shards of metal sliced through flesh that concerned every one of them. The statistics staggered the Marines. Fortunately, battlefield trauma was remarkably high tech, so one would have a better chance of surviving a blast than ever before. For some, though, the prospect of surviving was also unbearable. The general consensus was that it was better to die in a blast then go back home without arms and legs. Whether they really believed that was another story. It was part of the macho approach to dealing with death. It wasn't real yet. It was something they'd seen on the news. Day turned to night as they drove at a consistent 45 mph. They switched from driver, to turret gunner, to rest, and repeated the endless radio checks. A few vehicles broke down along the way. Each time a vehicle broke down, a frenzy of cordoned security and nervous excitement ensued.

The Marines always expected and were prepared for an ambush, but they hoped one never happened. They just never knew who was watching, waiting, and scheming. As riflemen, their place was on their feet. It was hard to get used to being such a big target. They appreciated the ride in a Humvee, but it was just too confined given the possibility of a lucky RPG shot. It was martial law and there were no cops. Indeed, they WERE the cops. Drive into oncoming traffic? No problem. Jump medians? Sure! Cause a traffic jam, slam into cars, and push them out of the way? Absolutely! Driving suspiciously and refusing to stop? That's a license to kill for a Marine. The urge to exercise that absolution was overwhelming. Overkill is an understatement. Just give these guys a reason.

After driving more than 36 hours, or over half way to their destination, the convoy pulled into a DOD (Department of Defense) installation to refuel and take care of necessary maintenance. They parked in long lines, parallel to each other in massive, parking lots filled with sand and rock. They set up a hasty camp in the limited space around their vehicles. This represented valuable time to get situated, grab some hot chow, check the scene, and link up with the guys to chat about the experience. They would stay for the night to ensure everyone had adequate rest for the remainder of the push, North. As the sun subsided, the men settled in with jokes and smokes. In those times, it's like a "get in where you fit in" mentality. Everyone seemed to become temporarily "cliqued up," marking territory, and always protecting unit integrity. They got used to the people in their company. This was also a perfect time for a trouble maker to go around and piss in their circles just to break up the monotony. This included trash-talk, Yo Momma jokes, and casual be-boppin' around, like being back on the block.

They carried their rifles everywhere they went. A solemn reminder hung from their shoulders by a fashioned piece of 550-cord. Complacency Kills! But for a moment, perhaps they could let their guard down a bit. With no watch scheduled for the night, it's right for any indulgence that one may find. Many of the Marines had bedded down. A couple of them were sitting around in their circles, shootin' the breeze. They were stretched out, adjacent to a separate convoy that had pulled in for the evening. It was an Army Reserve, Motor Transport Company from Kentucky. They were sitting around a big blue cooler. Their heavy-duty semi-trucks carried "Wide Loads" and were custom fitted with top-of-the-line stereo systems. "We drive all day, man, all around this fuckin' shit-hole country. Gotta have something to enjoy," one soldier said with a southern drawl. It was dark, late, and quiet. The moon shined bright in the clear night sky.

"Hey Doggie, whatcha got in that cooler?" He gave his Army buddies a questioning look, like "should I tell em'?" His buddy nodded and responded, "Shit man, they're Marines, they can probably smell that shit," he chuckled. "Well, since it's only two of ya. It's Iraqi Beer. You want one?" "What? Where'd you get that? Hell yeah!" the Marine exclaimed. The soldier was very calm and laid back. "Well, I brought the cooler from back home, we got the beers from a dude in the village outside the wire; it's black market shit. And we got the ice from the chow hall", he muttered with a smirk. Till this point, the Marines observed no indication this was a hostile environment. "Hey Sarent, check this out. These guys are offering us beers, what!" exclaimed one of the Marines. The Sergeant replied, "yeah shhhh, keep it down. Yeah man, pull up an MRE box." They introduced themselves, and one of the soldiers asked, "So where you guys headed?", "Haaa, we're not really at liberty to know or say - North," said the Marine. "Yeah...that little thing called OpSec, huh? Believe me, I'm not a grunt, but Hadgi knows what you're going to do before you do. They'll be watchin' and before long, they'll know your routine. It's unavoidable man, they hit us all the time with IEDs. They only got so many paved roads in this wasteland, but I ain't afraid to hop down and shoot some shit either," said the trucker, as a vein popped out of his head. The "snap-pop" of the can breaks the momentary silence, as they crack open their first cold beer in months. "Ahhhhh, what a fuckin' orgasm man! Thanks for looking out. Cheers!"

They toasted to everything and nothing - a rare exchange between two very different clubs. "So uh, what else can you get in that village," asked a Marine. "Like what," replied the trucker. "Something to chief on," answered the Marine. "Well, I got some brick. You want a pull?" The two Marines looked at each other and one said to the other, "not me...but you can go for it. Shit. You could die tomorrow. Just be ready to roll in the morning." The trucker pulled out a little one hitter from his breast pocket with a freshly packed bowl. With a single puff, the worm had turned, and tomorrow didn't matter. Induced by euphoric dreams, the war would wait another night. The next morning, they woke up groggy and sore from sleeping on top of the Humvees. Even before brushing their teeth, some of the guys packed in a chew to get a boost from the nicotine. The convoy mounted up and they were back on the road in a dispersed column of file.

They crossed the Euphrates River three times in the long, meandering trip through antiquity's Fertile Crescent. Night began to settle in again, as they neared the outskirts of Fallujah, a city infamous for recent intense fire fights. The closer they got to populated towns, the more pop shots they received from nearby houses and concealed positions. Shortly before their arrival into Camp Fallujah, a few of the senior NCOs (Non-Commissioned Officer) were designated to gather intelligence and make liaison with the battalion turning-over command of that AO. Their FOB (Forward Operating Base) was stationed in the same compound as the notorious Abu Ghraib Prison, the site of an unprecedented scandal for the US Government and alleged maltreatment of POWs (Prisoner of War). The convoy of Marines made radio contact and was granted clearance to pass through the obstacles, barricades, and barbed-wire. Looming overhead were heavy-machine gun emplacements with strategically employed fields of fire to cover the entire perimeter. The previous command had been there for 6 months, facing a hail of increased attacks, daily patrols, snipers, and a constant barrage of indirect mortar fire. They were "salty" and gave the new guys an earful of fucked up potential scenarios with the indigenous people that they would inevitably encounter. They were dirty with grime, the kind that can't be scrubbed off. Their faces were aged and they sported stocky statures, like venerated, old horses.

Their eyes were acute with unteachable knowledge and experience. Short-timers are on short time with only one thing in mind - going home. They handed over some maps and SOPs (Standard Operating Procedure) for the AO, some crucial lessons, and the rest was left up to them to figure out. It's a rite of passage for every unit, surviving the "new-in-country" sweepstakes. It's only earned through experience, time, and true grit and the short timers had no love for them. After they returned to the vehicles parked outside, they began to load up when the compound began receiving mortar fire. The rounds volleyed through the sky, whistling with remarkable force and fury. "Boom...Boom...Boom!", the steel rain descended upon and around the massive walls. The .50 caliber machine guns opened up on the town across the main MSR (Main Supply Route), from where the fire was usually suspected to come. The guys who had been there for a while remained very nonchalant about the whole affair. They laughed and joked at all the new guys scrambling around for cover amid the usual chaos. "Hey bro, no use in duckin' and weavin', they're coming from way-high in the sky. It's gonna drop where it drops" laughed a salty Marine. Just don't be there!" The attack lasted only minutes, as the concussions traveled through their organs and jiggled them all around. Everybody returned to their normal business following the all clear signal. "How is that normal," asked one Marine. The new guys just looked at each other in dismay. "Six more months of this shit," they grumbled. "Haaaa, yeah, that's if you don't get extended for three more months like we did, he said. "Hey, look Zaidan is a bitch," referring to the surrounding farmlands to the West of Fallujah. "Lock down your team leaders and get them accustomed to small unit missions because you're always gonna be spread thin. Don't worry guys, you'll get used to it...you'll figure it out." He concluded with an apathetic, "Semper Fucked!" It wasn't really the kind of positive advice they wanted to hear, but it rarely was.

The convoy detail continued toward Camp Fallujah with a different and more unsettling prospect for the future. They entered the compound of Camp Fallujah - a former Iraqi military installation, about six miles outside the City. The Marines linked up with the rest of company and were assigned to a group of large canvas tents near the corner of the base. Fatigued, many of them crawled to their bunk beds, and others meticulously organized their area. They were given the rest of their day to regroup, rest, and address continuous administrative and logistical issues. Unsurprisingly, there was not enough space to accommodate the battalion. They needed to extend beyond the lines, and create a new section of the camp. It required them to secure the area, set up a new perimeter, and clear it of UXOs, or unexploded ordinance, which was laden across large swaths of land used by Saddam's army. Heaps of debris and metal littered the landscape. This land would be their refuge in the weeks ahead.

Moke had been staying in contact with a buddy from back in their old unit in Hawaii, who was currently with 1st MAR DIV. Grover did his best to keep Moke and the other Marines informed. The two had sent correspondence back and forth in code through emails. OpSec (Operational Security) included information that the enemy could intercept online. Grover had been chosen from a "select few" who volunteered for special orders to deploy with a security detail from 1st MAR DIV, for the top brass. He left Hawaii 4 months before Charlie Company even had any idea they would be on the front lines of the Iraq War. Grover was a stud athlete. He was a leader with a rebellious streak, competitive, and intelligent. They all just wanted to get in the fight in 2004. Back then, they had to volunteer to get into the action. Today, a four year enlistment all but guarantees at least two combat deployments. When he heard Charlie Company had officially arrived to the Camp, Grover insisted on visiting the night they arrived, upon returning from a mission. He walked in, meandering familiar faces, with the typical unassuming look.

Like a reunion, they lined up to greet him, poke him for info, and assess the vibe from his veteran experience. It was good to see him, and it was quickly apparent, he was already a different man. Salty and vigilant, his gear was impeccably positioned on his person. An aura exuded from him, and it was humbling. It was the same feeling the Marines had during week 8 of boot camp as they gazed upon recruits transitioning to Marines, all the while knowing they had not experienced "The Crucible" yet. He stayed a while chatting with them. Before shaking hands and leaving, he said to Moke, "Hey, I'll probably see ya at the chow hall tomorrow", as he left the tent.

The next day, the Marines awoke and hustled around, completing the endless task of preparing gear lists and "Junk on the Bunk" (JOB) inspections to the point of redundancy. These countless inspections preceded every training, movement, or operation. Everyone was scattered in the tents or the space outside between the tents and the field expedient bathroom trailers. Suddenly, the Camp was hit in the southeast sector by a barrage of soviet-style 122mm, rocket fire. The first rocket screeched eerily as it traveled overhead, becoming louder as it dropped like a freight train from the sky. It went right over the tents and exploded with deafening concussion into the massive concrete barriers set up by the engineers. It ripped out chunks of concrete and tore through the adjacent tents' thin skin. Several people were wounded as chaos enveloped the scene. The Marines hit the deck, some throwing themselves from their top bunks, scrambling to grab their flak vest and helmet. They came pouring out of the tents, like stepping on an ant pile. Debris, dust and smoke filled the air. It took a few minutes for it to settle back to earth or be carried away with the wind. "Corpsman Up" was shouted from every direction.

The Marines immediately triaged the casualties - routine, priority, urgent. Their training kicked in with a tremendous shot of adrenaline. "Are we being attacked?" Expecting another attack, they grabbed their weapons and ran to sandbag emplacements and hasty, concrete bunkers. Some guys were still in their green silkies and shower shoes, vesturing a kevlar and flak. The rockets impacted several random positions within the Camp, including the MEC - a large motor pool for transport vehicles and Humvees. The individual squads then began account for their personnel and gear, known as an ACE report (Ammo, Casualties, and Equipment). Then, the violence subsided.

In sum, eight Marines were wounded in the attack, not including other areas of the camp that likely reported casualties. The attack critically wounded three Marines. They were immediately evacuated to Washington, D.C. by way of Germany, by way of Baghdad. The Navy Corpsman always had a remarkable ability to care for the Marines with whom they were imbedded. They have some of the sharpest minds on the battlefield. Simply put, they triage the casualties and save the lives that would have been otherwise lost to war's "natural causes." No one had died, so the assumption was they were extremely lucky and a sobering reality to how close they were to walk with death now. All the Marines retreated back to normal activity, feeling baptized by fire, pumped with adrenaline, wrestling each other, and arguing about who was scared. One Marine exclaimed, "You were scared motherfucker, I saw your asshole pucker up!" laughing obnoxiously. Even then, some are immune to wisdom and caution. The other Marine replied, "Hell yeah, I was scared. If you ain't scared, you're either a liar or fuckin' retarded."

Many of the small-unit leaders reassessed SOPs - what works best, and when. This first attack served as a teachable moment for all and a glimpse of their natural inclinations under fire. As absurd a concept as it is, the sooner the Marines got used to indirect fire and explosions in close proximity, the better off they would be the next time. They continued training for MOUT (Military Operations in Urban Terrain). They studied map overlays and constructed sand box terrain models, including targets and objectives. They rehearsed their missions and refined them over the next three weeks. It was critical that each Marine knew the others' jobs, and well enough to be effective if someone had to be replaced or a task performed. The small unit leadership of Marines makes or breaks a rifle squad.

The overall unit is a tool, glued together by the tight cohesion of its fire teams. These Marines are the guys actually fighting the wars every day, kicking in doors, and getting shot at. It's the real nitty-gritty. It is really where "the rubber meets the road" – by the soles of their boots. They were constantly drilled with the idea of discipline and preparation, using acronyms and brevity codes, pondering minutely fine details, and then executing it. The majority of the time, Plan A was completely scrapped in the first ten seconds of a mission, so there are always contingency plans in B and C. They say "Semper Gumby," or "Always Flexible," as their motto. It is the ability to adapt and overcome when the shit hits the fan, and do more with less, that are indicative to the skills that Marines have reluctantly mastered. They take great pride in this.

A few days had passed since the initial rocket attack in the Camp, and there was no word from Grover. Moke couldn't help but think that something had happened to him. Scuttlebutt was going around that the MEC was hit and someone was severely wounded and was medically evacuated out by helicopter. He tried not to dwell on it too much. Moke figured word would eventually trickle down, and the possibility was just too coincidental. After all, they had all just seen him the night before on their first day in Camp. It just didn't make sense how a guy with so much talent and potential could be so unlucky. These thoughts haunted Moke's mind, what if and why. They turned to other things because over-thought was not a friend. Basic comfort becomes a luxury and self-indulgence takes hold. They didn't want to lose those amenities. Each guy has to accept things in their own way, but ultimately they had to rely on each other, regardless of personal conflict. Their lives and future were at stake. If it didn't kill them, it would make them stronger.

Zaidan, Iraq October 2004

A few weeks prior to the "re-invasion of Fallujah" kicking off, 1st Battalion, 3rd Marines were assigned to a particular AO (Area of Operation), mainly conducting mounted patrols, 24 hour React Force missions, feints, and short deployments within the outer farmlands of Zaidan, in the al Anbar Province. The units were getting accustomed to the environment, the feel around civilians, certain trends or oddities. It was such a foreign place to them, the smells, things burning, the arid air combined with the blistering heat of the day. Charlie Company was tasked with pushing out into the rural surroundings to execute their presence, patrol, gather intel, and potentially disrupt enemy activity and supply lines near the Euphrates River. The environment quickly changed from dry dust to lush green fields, irrigated by a system of canals. Goats roamed and people lived on a level of meager subsistence, never imagined by the average American. Palm and Date Trees sporadically sprouted from the ground for shade. People came out from their houses to witness the spectacle of US forces trampling through their fields, in awe and disgust. Suspicion and paranoia infected both sides. Neither side understood the other. They may have shared the same basic human characteristics, but the two sides could not have been more culturally distinct.

The Marine infantry units consisted mostly of teenagers and very young adults – kids really. They grew up watching their heroes in war movies about WWII and Vietnam. They also grew up believing in the "American Dream" and the liberty to choose one's own path. Meanwhile, their counterparts lived under religious oppression, the commands of dictators, tribal law, little to no education, virtually no money, and limited access to information and current events. Essentially, these people, "the enemy", lived in the same way as they had for hundreds of years. Most of the Marines felt like they had stepped back in time.

The Marines patrolled for hours, from the middle of the night, to mid-day, and often into night again. The muddy fields had been caked onto their cammies and filled every bit of tread on the soles of their boots. Each step seemed like carrying cinder blocks on their feet. Movement became cumbersome with all of the gear, and most became extremely fatigued. But this was no time to be weak. The unit had little resupply options for the patrol, so command cautioned the Marines to conserve their water. As it turned out, their mission was a low priority for logistical support, because of increased attacks from IEDs and VBIEDs (Vehicle–Borne IEDs) on American convoys. The patrol proceeded slowly and without major incident. After a few days and nights slogging through canals and fields, the allure began to lose its flavor. They succumbed to that scourge of complacency and boredom. They took breaks slumped up against a rock pile wall as a humid mist burned away from the sun's radiation. A few of them drifted asleep as soon as their ass hit solid ground. They learned how to sleep in the most uncomfortable positions, exhausted, thirsty, and hungry.

After only a few minutes, they awoke with a groggy, return to reality. They were all wet and disoriented, not knowing how much time had passed during their slumber. They began to appreciate the danger posed by simple fatigue. The more tired they became, the less effective they could fight. Times like these quickly forced these young warriors to question which fate awaited them in the days and weeks ahead. After three days in Zaidan, most of the Marines had drunk all the water they could carry and began filling their canteens from the irrigation canals. While generally known to be fraught with bacteria, the dirty canal water satisfied their need to quench their thirst. They decontaminated as much of their water as they could with iodine tablets. Otherwise, the extreme heat would have literally cooked their brains in their skulls. Mixed with the iodine, the water tasted similar to metal and still did not guarantee they would not later contract some terrible disease. Meanwhile, they received no news about when resupply would arrive, or when they would return to Camp.

In the distance, several IEDs exploded sporadically throughout the days, as plumes of smoke climbed above the tree line. Their war was approaching quickly, but it still seemed far away and there was reluctance to embracing any feeling of comfort. Complacency kills, and they all needed to fight through those moments to remain vigilant and aware when it seemed appropriate to kick back and relax. After a few days, the Marines from Charlie Company returned back to the Camp. Not surprisingly, many of the guys came down with a 24-hour viral infection from drinking the water, but fortunately none were prevented from continuing on with the mission. They mostly just puked, shit diarrhea, and gave into nature's fury until the bug ran its course through their bodies.

The invasion was close. It was scheduled for the following week, but Washington politics would hold sway over the final decision to go, until the results of the 2004 Presidential Race were tallied up, between the incumbent and the Democratic nominee. The grunts were getting bits of information about the outside world from journalists and reporters that were embedded in the Camp, reporting on the developing assault of Fallujah. The Marines didn't care to get wrapped up in the politics of it too much. They just "kept it simple-stupid" or KISS. They viewed this moment as an opportunity to hunt and kill bad guys, and feel the rush of a worthy proving ground. They trained for war. They trained to kill. They committed to protecting their brothers. They were prepared to die, but they hoped to survive. This was their business.

Gearing up for Invasion

The Marines spent the last couple weeks prior to the invasion cramming information into their brains. They constructed more sand models of the city, ran through every scenario, and trained for the foreseeable. Six months ago, they were patrolling with blanks in their rifles, in the mountains of Hawaii. Now they would invade a fortified city in middle of the Iraqi, desert. In terms of urban combat, they were grossly unprepared, except for their pure grit.

Meanwhile, Command withheld the most critical information on a "need-to-know" basis. This generally served two purposes - it maintains OpSec and it really pisses people off. The logic being that the Marines will be so irritated and angry when they finally reveal the news about the mission, that they'll charge machine guns and jump on grenades in a furious rage. Keeping Marine grunts mad and hungry, has always served America well and their enemies poorly. The whole reason for being there in the first place was an enigma, mostly fueled by the ambitions of one man...Mad Mike.

Battalion Commander Mad Mike seized the perfect opportunity within his realm of authority. The MEU provided him enough flexibility to position the battalion to win a coveted spot in the Fallujah Assault. Mad Mike engaged a distinguished Pentagon contact list, and ultimately punched the ticket needed for the MEU to become an integral part of the operation. Thus, the MEU brought all of its assets to the front lines. The Marines all knew Mad Mike had meticulously planned this well in advance. For a battalion commander, it was as much a career move as it was the defining moment for the Lava Dawgs as a unit. Marines and soldiers alike could serve 20 years in the military and never get that opportunity again.

Those who didn't participate in the assault would have a sour taste in their mouths for years to come. The remarkable diversity of the Marine Corps would be represented. There was a plethora of supporting elements operating all across the Fallujah area. In terms of infantry units, First Battalion, Third Marines (1/3) would be an unanticipated addition to the conflict. They deployed as an expeditionary unit and performed what was, historically, the indigenous mission of the Marine Corps. First Battalion, Third Marines (1/3) represented Hawaii. First Battalion, Eighth Marines (1/8) represented the East Coast. Third Battalion, Fifth Marines (3/5), and Third Battalion, First Marines (3/1) represented the West Coast. For the 31st MEU and 1/3, the operation presented an extraordinary challenge of logistics to deploy so far inland and contribute to the massive assault bearing down on Fallujah. For the last year, all the "fuck-fuck games" had led them to this point. There was no stopping the inevitable.

One late October day, the men gathered around during some down time. They discussed shared expectations. They downplayed their fear. They focused on pulling their own weight when the time came, and not costing anyone their life. The officer ranks within Charlie Company suffered a minor rift. It seemed higher command had issues with the commander of First Platoon. They would later be dubbed "The Black Sheep". Lt. K-9, the platoon commander, was nothing like what his nickname would suggest. The Chicago native was quiet and unpretentious, but steady and confident. He embraced their image as the bastard children of Charlie Corps. He molded his platoon into better warriors and earned the men's respect. However, his leadership was brought into question after an earlier incident in Zaidan. It was hard to fathom that without warrant, a unit commander could be so easily expendable. From a combat standpoint, Fallujah was the Super Bowl, and that's like benching the starting quarterback for whole game, just for throwing an incomplete pass.

To lose command or responsibility within the ranks can be devastating, both for the person being relieved and the unit that they commanded. The company leadership completely ignored the negative ramifications of that. In the competitive military world of careers and egos, there was no mercy. A few days prior to the invasion, the company elite relieved K-9 of his duties and quietly discarded him. The Command largely based its decision of the fact that an Engineer detachment got themselves lost while patrolling with Charlie Company in Zaidan. They were attached to K-9's platoon and the responsibility was, ultimately, placed on his shoulders, even if those dumb ass Engineers couldn't navigate or follow the guy in front of them.

The Command swiftly moved K-9 to the Headquarters S-3 shop and replaced him with Preacher, a staff non-commissioned officer. Ironically, months earlier, Preacher's command fired him as a Weapons Company platoon sergeant, for overall weakness and incompetence. K-9 and Preacher effectively switched positions. This represented an unusual move, considering the Platoon Commander slot was reserved for an officer, unfitting of a SNCO (Staff Non Commissioned Officer), except in the tragic event that the officer was killed in combat. Command fired a highly competent and respected officer days before a platoon of impressionable "kids" engaged in their first taste of combat. Many of the Marines felt Preacher's promotion reflected the Command's lack of competence and commitment to their welfare – an already complex and dangerous environment made more unpredictable by the dubious decision of an unlikely Marine, Capt. Quiet. Quiet was a desk jockey in Headquarters at the cusp of his career. He was elevated to the CO (Commanding Officer) billet after the entire command structure of the company was demoted and replaced, including the Company Gunnery Sergeant, First Sergeant, XO, etc. This made matters worse, because the battalion was already stretched thin during to the death of a Marine PFC, during a training evolution.

The fallen was a young Marine who collapsed of heat exhaustion during training in Okinawa. Nobody could have predicted or prevented his unfortunate death. Nonetheless, his tragic passing served as the catalyst for dramatic, pre-war, restructuring. Investigations fell upon 3rd Marines from the highest level of the NIS (Naval Investigative Service). The Marines knew heads would roll, and someone would be blamed. There were even rumors of negligent homicide charges. The events inevitably set off a shockwave of events exemplary of the hierarchical and political structure of the military. Someone fucked up and a training evolution went awry, resulting in a death. The higher command fired the lower. People pointed fingers. Careers were ruined. Shit rolled downhill. Semper Gumby!

October 30, 2004

Word started to trickle down from other units that a 7-ton transport truck from Bravo Company had been hit by a suicide VBIED (Vehicle-Borne, Improvised Explosive Device). Eight Marines and a Navy Corpsman lost their lives, and eleven more were wounded in the attack. Bravo was running QRF (Quick Reaction Force) missions and mounted patrols around the city. For Battalion 1/3, the attack accounted for the largest loss of life up to that point. Casualties were mounting from skirmishes with enemy forces and their suspected sympathizers. Other non-combat Humvee accidents claimed others' health and ability to fight. Marines were already dying and the battle had not yet begun! Their minds raced with "who was it" and "do I know them?" The living reflected on things left undone, memories, and the unknown. It was a brutal awakening to the carnage they faced ahead of them. The fallen Bravo Company Marines were remembered for their personal character and sacrifice. They are listed below:

Bravo Company KIA – October 30, 2004

Lance Cpl. John T. Byrd, 23, Fairview, WV
Lance Cpl. Jeremy D. Bow, 20, Lemoore, CA
Sgt. Kelley L. Courtney, 28, Macon, GA

Lance Cpl. Travis A. Fox, 25, Cowpen, SC
Cpl. Christopher J. Lapka, 22, Peoria, AZ
Pfc. John Lukac, 19, Las Vegas, NV
Pfc. Andrew G. Reidel, 20, Northglenn, CO
Lance Cpl. Michael P. Scarborough, 28, Washington, GA

The Marines of Charlie Company bedded down for the night with a concrete roof overhead, and sand bags filled the window spaces. Inside, there was a sense of ease. These precious moments provided time to catch up on anything important, like sleep. Darkness descended as the artillery battery fired successive volleys into the night, impacting their targets in the City miles away. The sound of outgoing fire is calming, because it is not incoming. It provided the Marines with some solace. It gave them a temporary blanket for the REM-inducing effects of an unconscious slumber.

A couple days before the Marines crossed into the City, various units departed the Camp in AmTrac vehicles and tanks to conduct feint operations. This consisted of probing into different parts of the city to lure enemy contact, gain intel, and keep the insurgency off-balanced. The city was more or less a rectangle shape. U.S. forces could theoretically have invaded from any or all sides. These couple days provided an opportunity to poke their heads out of the top of the AmTrac to get a good look of the City. It looked ominous; inciting visions of glory, vengeance, and nothingness.

They would move forward, make contact with small arms and RPG blasts. They would acquire targets, return fire, and mark for future missions. The AmTracs would drop the back hatches, Marines would pour out, and secure the outlying area. They would search and secure unexplored places like junkyards, cemeteries, and car depots, where caches of weapons were stored. And they would disrupt enemy observations posts on the edges of the city. The area around the Cloverleaf was always a hot bed for activity, sizzling with IEDs and ambushes. The Cloverleaf represented a main route for highway traffic and offered the enemy convenient escape routes back into the city. Finally, they would mount back up and try to kill some time, spit a dip, or write a letter. On the final night before the assault, those Marines that could sleep spent their final hours sprawled out in their racks. Others spent their time talking and reminiscing. In the early morning of November 8, laden with gear, the Marines crammed into the AmTracs and pushed out to the LOD (Line of Departure). Phantom Fury had begun!

Chapter 3

Happy Birthday to Us

Nov. 10 2004...Phase Line Charles...North of Phase Line Fran

The sun began to peek over the rooftops as the Marines seized the morning and moved with a sense of urgency. Intel flowed through the radio and those in charge relayed "the word" to the unit leaders. Security posts from the prior night were relieved by replacements and hostile activity was evident in the neighborhood. But, this day was like no other. It was the 229th Birthday of the Marine Corps. Most Marines not deployed to a combat zone anxiously anticipated the festivities that accompanied the tradition. Those Marines likely laced up in ballrooms, beverages in hand, standing in front of mirrors, meticulously scrutinizing their Dress Blue uniforms to satisfy an impeccable standard. This day was ingrained in their brains as a shrine, a reminder of the tradition and values that existed before them. Blood was spilled and the Marine Corps reputation was fiercely upheld for over two centuries. To some degree, this fact was inspiring the Marines in Fallujah.

The Sergeant Major of the battalion (highest ranking enlisted man) drove through the streets playing "The Marine Corps Hymn" and "the National Anthem" from loudspeakers retro-fitted to the roof of a Humvee. This act infuriated the Mujahadeen (foreign, Islamic) fighters, so naturally the Marines used it as a tactic to draw the enemy out into the streets to fight. The insurgents despised hearing American music and the audacious display of the Infidels' arrogance. The Sgt. Major made periodic stops to congratulate the Marines on their advances and offered a few motivating words to mark the occasion. It is the tradition for the oldest and the youngest Marine to toast to the first piece of cake. In this case, an MRE pound cake with a candle atop sufficed - a field-expedient version.

The Marine Corps Birthday presented a time to reflect on the things that made the Corps special. Leaders utilized the holiday to regurgitate famous quotes or introduce a few historic words of their own. At its core, the Birthday always connected the old and the new breeds of Marines. Old Marines hoped that it would forever remind the younger generations what it required to build and what it will demand to endure. To know what it means to hold the title of Marine, especially in the midst of the current circumstances in Fallujah, served as a rallying cry, an exuberant feeling of motivation.

Many of the Marines downplayed the highest level of "Ooh-Rah-ness," but they couldn't help but feel immense pride in their purpose. They knew of the historic nature of the current operation, but did not quite fully appreciate its magnitude. The rare opportunity led to an unquestionable paradox the grunts faced that day, and each subsequent day in Fallujah. High on adrenaline and vigorously living the best of life; they also needed to accept that on the same day, they might lose it all while skirting the edge of legends. A fight like Fallujah only comes around every 40 or 50 years. Most men would prefer to be remembered when they die, but to die as a Marine, on this day, would be extraordinarily honorable.

First Platoon patrolled and secured the area around the temporary CP (Command Post) when the Marines on watch began to shout and holler. The Marines fired their weapons and chaos ensued. Two Marines in particular, Razor and Blade, ran to the front of the CP brandishing their SAWs (Squad Automatic Weapon), as a suspected enemy fighter approached from down the street. He was wearing a blue sweat suit and white sneakers. He was shot in the leg and bled on the street, yet smiled with a sinister grin as he walked nonchalantly towards Razor and Blade. They yelled, "STOP" in Arabic several times, and signaled him to get on the ground. The wounded insurgent refused. Instead, he continued to walk towards them, ignoring their commands with an eerie smile on his face. Suddenly, he reached down into the crotch of his pants. Immediately, a vigorous 10-round burst from the Marines entered his head and chest, as he fell limp to the ground. They witnessed the life leave his eyes before he was parallel to the deck.

The event was nothing like the movies, when the victim gets thrown back 20 feet. The body just lost all motor function and collapsed on itself; falling in the direction of the projectile, lifeless. Razor was stunned how easy it was to end a life. He and Blade jumped up and trotted back to the lines. The incident happened so fast. In seconds, the Marines analyzed a threat, executed and escalated the continuum of force, and followed the rules of engagement on a target. From this point forward, they presumed there remained no innocent men in the city. All locals had ample opportunity to leave with their lives and family, as the US forces dropped leaflets warning people to evacuate weeks before. As such, most civilians, especially women and children, fled before the invasion. Clearly, the city was empty, except for insurgent fighters.

This phenomenon was somewhat unprecedented. Civilian casualties were fortunately very low-to-none with respect to past offensive operations of this magnitude. But when the Brass cut the Marines loose in the beginning of the fight, simply put, the Marines steam rolled everything between them and their objective.

During the initial days of battle, military-aged males who decided to stay were fair game according to the ROEs, regardless of their intent. Reports indicated several snipers would shoot at Marines, drop their weapons in a house, and walk across the street to another vantage point where another weapon was stored – repeat. In the first few days of the heaviest fighting, no chances were taken.

Later that night, AmTracs and Humvees doing resupply runs repeatedly rolled over the dead corpses in the street, opening up a gaping holes in their head. Later, stray dogs devoured their brains and fought to pick apart the exposed flesh. Bull and his fire team were sitting around a circle of chemlights, eating MREs. "Aggghhhh, the cycle of life is complete. You popped your fuckin' cherry today, huh Blade," exclaimed Bull with a laugh. "I'll trade you a grape jelly for your jalapeño cheese?"

The Command widely dispersed the platoons of Charlie Company, and tasked each with specific missions for the day of November 10th. Second platoon controlled the far right flank, assisting Bravo Company. During the previous few days, the Marines became well aware of the surrounding areas. They stressed an acute awareness regardless of the situation, and had studied every nook and cranny while on guard and patrol.

As he stood watch on the rooftop of the temporary patrol base across from the mosque, Moke worried that Soup and Rasta's squads would likely encounter heavy hostility. Generally, the further to the West they ventured, the more resistance they encountered. He knew that Second Platoon had just moved west, and he had a bad feeling about the two insurgents that escaped at the bizarre on the first day. He remembered them running down the same street to the South with RPGs and medium machine guns. They likely regrouped in the most structurally sound house they could find. Second Platoon would surely make contact with them during the sweep with Bravo Company.

Determining whether certain houses or buildings were attractive to insurgent occupation or activity became second nature to the Marines. Each side sought to capitalize on the same limited resources and strategic locations. High buildings and rooftops providing an observation advantage, strong support structures providing cover, and clear avenues of approach for good fields of fire took priority. The enemy would inevitably draw them in as close as possible or attempt to funnel them into traps. The Marines presumed their enemy would never be so bold as to attempt to assault and take control of a structure the Marines occupied.

House-to-house fighting seemed suicidal for many reasons, and boasted a casualty rate of 60% or higher. Rarely, would the insurgents attempt ambushes from street level unless they first coordinated with IED attacks and there existed convenient escape routes. The Marines understood that the enemy could only fight a war of attrition and hope to inflict as much damage as possible. The insurgents would normally fight from defensive positions, barricaded in a back room with a view of the top of a stairway. This provided an ideal choke point and kill zone, as doorways, hallways, and stairwells were usually dark or dimly lit. The unknown spawned a constant fear. The Marines quickly realized the realities of urban combat. No other battlefield compares.

Charlie Company, Second Platoon - Ambush House

As the Marines cleared the blocks of houses in support of Bravo Company, Second Platoon, Charlie Company began receiving sniper fire from adjacent buildings. To achieve a foothold, they advanced by squads into two houses separated by an alleyway. Rasta's squad entered one way into the left house and Soup Can's squad into the other to the right. Soup made entry into a large house, partially unfinished, as many of them were. They began clearing the bottom rooms as they had several times before, each fire team taking a room. The house contained a large open space in the middle, with a stairwell that wrapped along the wall and up to the second level. There were no railings, which was unusual to the senses, and incited a temporary feeling of vertigo.

After the first level of the house was deemed clear, First Fire Team stacked on the wall. Pick, Gonzo, Smiley, and Zob steadily ascended the stairway. Pick and Gonzo both carried SAWs at the ready. Their light machine guns could spit out 200 rounds in 10 seconds. The open stairway dangerously exposed them to enemy fire with nowhere to go except up or down, and gravity worked against them. Pick was a confident and exuberant, 20-year old from Illinois. He led his squad, charging up the stairs with his SAW in hand. As he made the turn to clear a room to the right, he walked directly into a machine gun bunker that insurgents had set up in the back of the room, fixed directly on the doorway. The enemy machine gun riddled Pick from head to toe, instantly dropping him to the floor. Gonzo was directly behind him and also received four rounds to his leg and hip from the Soviet-made machine gun. The inertia of the gunfire threw Gonzo back off his feet and there was nothing to break his fall. He fell over the side of the stairwell about 20 feet to the floor below. As he fell, the force took Smiley and Zob along with him.

Gonzo hit the ground with a loud "THUD!" The weight of his gear and his momentum came to bear down on his body. Smiley wasn't hit and landed like a cat on his hands and feet, then hugging the wall underneath the stairwell. Zob had fallen back down the stairway, while firing his rifle. He was hit twice – one that penetrated a 40mm grenade strapped to his vest, and one that hit his gas mask. Luckily, he was completely unscathed. He regressed into a fury, cursing those "Motherfuckers!!!" He propped himself up and fired a 40mm grenade from his M203 launcher, only to see it ricochet off the walls and land on the deck. It didn't have enough distance to arm itself and explode. Fighting in those confined spaces was deafening to everyone, combined with the shell-shocking moments of exploding fragmentation grenades. There was a tremendous amount of hot metal flying everywhere. Marines were screaming.

The intensity of the gunfire was relentless. The rooms were filled with powdery dust and smoke from the grenades exploding. Everyone could taste the Composition B in their mouths. The soot combined with their saliva and blackened their teeth. Gonzo bled and screamed for Pick. All hell broke loose and Pick was unresponsive. The enemy coordinated their fire and had positioned themselves perfectly. They had 90 degrees of cover from an angled wall that completely shielded them from the Marines' onslaught. They would poke their heads out and shoot down, limiting their exposure. Soup and Smiley dragged Gonzo into a nearby room as Doc House began treating his bullet wounds.

Four to five insurgent fighters remained nested in the back room. They enjoyed the angle on the Marines and began chucking grenades down on them, two and three at a time. The concussive explosions were consecutive, concurrent, and everything in between. Soup Can's squad fired back, expending hundreds of rounds into the walls. The Marines found themselves in a precarious position that eliminated their ability to throw grenades up to dislodge the enemy fighters, because the 90 degree angle of the room provided virtually no angle from which to aim from below. The only way to achieve an angle was to expose themselves on the stairwell, but that was suicidal. Soup was on the hand-held radio, trying to relay a SitRep (Situation Report) to his platoon commander. A few blocks away, the Lieutenant was unaware of the severity of his platoon's situation. The squad was pinned down as the fighting continued. Shell casings littered the ground.

Several minutes later, Rasta brought his squad to make entry into the ambush house and reinforce the other squad. Rasta stacked up on the wall with Blitz and Mort. They made entry, as Soup yelled, "Watch out!" A rapid burst from an AK-47 chipped away at the ground following their steps. They jumped for cover and crawled up against the protection of the walls. After throwing themselves into the fray, they quickly realized that they were pinned down too. It was a trap to get them sucked into the kill zone. They had to retrieve Pick's body, which was still lying lifeless atop the stairs. Knowing they would never leave their buddies behind, the insurgent's clever scheme was taking its toll as the wounded began to accumulate. Lifer came on scene with members from his squad in Third Platoon, including Snoop Doc. They came to reinforce and treat the wounded.

As they ran down the alleyway separating the two houses towards the casualties, the insurgents fired down upon them with AK-47s, killing Snoop Doc instantly. The 22-year old Navy Corpsman from Florida, had volunteered to go help the wounded. His fellow Marines loved him and they affectionately coined him with the name because he resembled the famous rapper. Lifer found himself in shock. It happened so fast. He returned fire as he and other Marines dragged Snoop Doc's body around the corner to the rear of the house. He was already gone. Every time they would move to get position or help the wounded, the enemy gunfire would reinvigorate. Rasta shouted, "frag out" in a loud Jamaican accent, as he pulled the pin on a grenade and hurled it at the insurgents.

The grenade bounced off a few a walls and back down the stairway. Sounding like, "Clink, clink, clink," as it rolled down each step, back towards them. The Marines curled up in the fetal position, covering their ears and opening their mouths to lessen the pressure of the blast. The grenade didn't go off! It still had the thumb clip secured around the spoon, which served as an extra safety mechanism. As far as blunders go, this was a fortunate one. "Fuck," screamed Rasta, as he ran back out to retrieve and throw it again. The second attempt exploded near the bunkered room. Again, the gunfire intensified as Soup called in a MedEvac for the wounded. It was loud and confusing. Specs ran through the kill zone to get to a better position, and he was raked by gunfire in the arm. He found cover in a room, attempting to treat himself.

The desperate fight continued for more than an hour, and the confidence of the men slowly dwindled. Blitz continued firing and reloading, exposing himself around corners with drum after drum of ammo from his SAW, each containing 200 rounds. The barrel was hot and smoking. He was frustrated because he knew he had hit the enemy fighters a few times, but they just kept firing back at him. Blitz took a second to reload, crouching down on a knee, becoming infuriated by the screams from his comrades. He ran low on ammo. Firmly clutching his SAW, he looked down at his weapon as beads of sweat rolled off his nose, splashing on the linked 5.56mm ammo. Smiley yelled to him, but they couldn't see each other. Blitz poked his head out to see where his fellow Marines were. He struggled to hear them in all the confusion, but they were scattered throughout the bottom level by this time. Suddenly, one of the insurgents appeared from around the corner, firing at him from merely a few feet away.

As bullets whizzed past Blitz's head, he could see the spiraling rotation as they impacted the walls behind him. He raised his SAW and filled the insurgent with a 20-round burst. The enemy's blood splattered onto Blitz's face as the lifeless body slumped into a contorted position against the wall. Blitz kept firing and was enraged as his SAW jammed from the ceaseless expense of ammunition. His veins filled with adrenaline, his heart seemed to beat out of his chest, as he tried to catch his breath.

Mort and Rasta were still pinned down on the opposite side, separated by the large room in the center of the fight, which became the kill zone. They refused to switch places to relieve him. Instead they tossed Blitz their weapons when he ran out of ammunition. Time and sound ceased to exist. His natural instincts took over. His vision tunneled, and he took a deep breath. He grabbed two grenades after having some fellow team member pull the pins. With a grenade in each hand, Blitz made another charge towards the bunkered room, launching the grenades.

Meanwhile, the rest of the platoon was scattered outside the walls of the house, trying to formulate a plan to outflank and neutralize the enemy threat. The lieutenant flagged down a D9 Bulldozer that had been clearing debris and constructing barriers on the roads and intersections. It was fully armored, and the Marine driving the D9 also carried a rifle, and knew how to use it. The lieutenant ordered the driver to knock down the corner of the building where the insurgents were barricaded. The rattling sounds came, "Clank, Clank, Clank," as the solid metal tracks grinded into the ground. The D9 maneuvered up to the ambush house and crashed the front-end shovel into the building. Inside the house, Blitz and the rest of Second Platoon were still enthralled in the fight. Suddenly, the walls and the roof came crashing down on them.

The driver immediately reversed the dozer. The D9's movement revealed the insurgents and Marines inside, virtually on top of one another. One particular insurgent found himself between Iraq and a hard place, hanging from the spike of the D9's massive shovel. The driver immediately realized and slammed it down to the deck, crushing the insurgent underneath. Next, he opened the hatch and shot him a few more times with his M-16 to make sure. The wall had crumbled on top of Gonzo, Blitz, and Mort, covering them in rubble. Soup, Rasta, Zob, and the others rushed to remove the huge pieces of concrete from the trapped Marines. Additionally, they seized the opportunity to recover Pick's dead body from the top of the stairs. After several minutes of removing the rocks and debris, the wounded Marines were extracted.

The falling building crushed Blitz. He suffered a fractured shoulder and femur. His case was especially critical because the injuries compromised a main artery which runs along the leg. A Corpsman placed a tourniquet around his leg. If it was punctured, he could've died within minutes from losing so much blood. Mort's ankle was also smashed from the collapsed wall. Gonzo and Specs were wounded by gunfire and bled profusely. Soup assisted with the MedEvac when the AmTracs pulled up. They began to load all the wounded. As he was being evacuated on a litter and high on morphine, Gonzo grabbed the arm of the Company First Sergeant as he passed by. In a thick Puerto Rican accent, he reminded him, "I want my two beers, First Sergeant, I didn't forget!" He referred to the pre-invasion covenant that each Marine would receive two beers on Christmas. The small things made the biggest difference over there.

The First Sergeant instantly felt a heavy heart, responding, "Son, you deserve much more than that," as they carried Gonzo away. The scene quieted down, but they were not fully convinced the bunkered room was annihilated. Beats, an assault man, came running up with a high explosive SMAW (Shoulder-launched Multipurpose Assault Weapon). He launched it into the remainder of the house, obliterating the rest of the second level. The house that stood that morning was completely demolished by mid-day. It was Second Platoon's first up close encounter with the enemy. The day's battle left 2 KIAs (Killed in Action), including 4 enemy KIAs, and several WIAs (Wounded in Action). Some of the wounded would never return to the platoon.

For his actions in commanding his squad and assisting in the MedEvac of several Marines, Soup Can was awarded the Navy and Marine Corps Commendation Medal with Valor. The events of that day would propel them into Marine Corps History. It was an eerie feeling to be engaged in such a terrible fight on their birthday, due to the historical significance. One of the first things a recruit learns is the founding birthday of the Corps. The twisted reality of the engagement made the fight instantly legendary, at least in their minds. Without glorifying a tragedy, the men who sacrificed their lives on November 10 would proudly confirm its significance, as it lay embedded in stone next to their names. The deaths of Pick and Snoop Doc sent a ripple through the battalion. They were among the first from 1/3 to be killed in action since the invasion began.

KIA: November 10, 2004

Lance Cpl. Aaron C. Pickering, 20, Marion, IL
Petty Officer 3rd Class, Julian Woods, 22, Jacksonville, FL

For his heroic and selfless action in the defense of his fellow Marines, and ultimately counter-attacking an enemy ambush and driving them back to allow the platoon to regroup while also being wounded as a result of the fighting, Blitz was awarded the Silver Star, the third highest award for gallantry in combat.

Just days before the invasion, the battalion had received a shipment of mail. Moke got a letter from a friend back in Hawaii. Inside of it was a laminated prayer from the Bible called Psalms 91. He wasn't a religious man. He even scoffed at the notion of having faith in a supreme being. Written above the prayer, there was a passage explaining the significance of that particular verse. During WWI, some of the fiercest trench warfare in history was being fought across Europe in places like Belleau Wood and the Argonne Forest. A unit of the US Army known as the 91st Infantry Brigade, most of them conscripted and inexperienced in combat, adopted the practice of reciting the prayer every day while in front-line combat. While many units suffered up to 90-percent casualty rates, unverified accounts indicate that no member of the 91st Brigade was ever killed or wounded.

Some research disputes the fact that the 91st Brigade even existed, but none of the Marines knew that at the time. There was no way to verify it, but it sounded good. It wouldn't hurt to be a little superstitious. Maybe it didn't matter if it was true. All that mattered was their collective faith in it. Moke was skeptical, but he was enticed by history. He thought about all the guys in his squad, some were Christians, some were not. However, he knew the power of the written word. If it made some of the guys feel better, it couldn't hurt to have a little extra momentum. In previous "wars of attrition," it was said "there are no atheists in a fox hole." Faith is like an invisible shield. If a person really believes that they are protected, then they are. If nothing else, it offered them comforting words when their lives were in jeopardy. Following a unanimous decision, they adopted the practice themselves and recited the verse before every mission. Many of them carried a copy in their helmets and took turns reading it each day. It became as much a psychological advantage as a way to forge unity amongst the squad.

Psalms 91

He who dwells in the secret place of the Most High
Shall abide under the shadow of the Almighty
I will say of the Lord "He is my refuge and my fortress"
My God in Him I will trust
Surely He shall deliver you from the snare of the fowler
And from the perilous pestilence
He shall cover you with His feathers
And under His wings you shall take refuge
His truth shall be your shield and buckler
You shall not be afraid of the terror by night
Nor of the arrow that flies by day
Nor of the pestilence that walks in darkness
Nor of the destruction that lays waste at noonday
A thousand may fall at your side
And ten thousand at your right hand
But it shall not come near you
Only with your eyes shall you look
And see the reward of the wicked
Because you have made the Lord who is my refuge

Even the Most High your habitation
No evil shall befall you
Nor shall any plague come near your dwelling
For He shall give His angels charge over you
To keep you in all your ways
They shall bear you up in their hands
Lest you dash your foot against a stone
You shall tread upon the lion and the cobra
The young lion and the serpent you shall trample underfoot
Because he has set his love upon Me
Therefore I will deliver him
I will set him on high because he has known My name
He shall call upon Me and I will answer him
I will be with him in trouble
I will deliver him and honor him
With long life I will satisfy him
And show him My salvation.

November 11, 2004 - Charlie Company, First Platoon

In an effort to further secure their patrol base perimeter, First Squad set out to clear an adjacent house in which they had heard movement. Moke and Wildo took a sniper and M240 machine gunner to the roof. The fire teams made entry as they blasted the corners and windows of the building with grenade and machine gun fire. Inside, they found a lone insurgent curled up in a corner, crying. They found 3 AK-47s, several rounds, and plastic bags full of prescription drugs. Pepe, Groucho, and Weed detained the EPW (Enemy Prisoner of War) without firing another shot. Pepe was a young, 19-year old boot, but a natural warfighter. He carried a shot gun as a secondary breaching weapon. His gear was impeccable and his maturity, discipline, and tactical mindset were rare for his age and experience. He covered their exit, as the team led the EPW out the house, blindfolded and past a mound of dirt that had been pushed up by the D9 dozer to block a roadway. Jutting from the top of the dirt was a pair of legs from a dead insurgent. They were stiff, straight with rigor mortis. As the Marines often interpret war on the ground with dark humor, they nicknamed him "Crazy Legs."

The day yielded some minor casualties and the acquisition of more EPWs. During an overzealous firefight that night, First Platoon evacuated a Marine who had suffered some rocks in his eye, resulting from the "back-blast" of an AT-4 (anti-tank weapon) as it was fired on a suspected insurgent hideout. The back-blast is a vacuum of pressure that is propelled from the back of a shoulder-fired rocket. If standing behind it, a Marine can suffer severe injury as debris can become shrapnel. It took a full team of four Marines to carry Remy's 6'5", 240 lb. frame to the MedEvac. To think about losing an eye, or any body part for that matter, haunted them. The reality kicked in that they were just as dangerous to themselves as the enemy was. Then, they started to think too much. Their training taught them right from wrong and the DOs and DON'Ts, but combat produces something else – trial by fire -- and the situation dictates. Their inexperience bred uncertainty. Mistakes were inevitable.

November 12, 2004 - Bravo Company

In the hours between dawn and dusk, two more "Lava Dawg" Marines were killed during combat operations in the East Manhattan AO. As they cleared several houses and valiantly engaged the enemy, Lance Corporal David M. Branning, 21, Cockesville, Maryland and Lance Corporal Brian A. Medina, 20, Woodbridge, VA, succumbed to enemy grenades and rifle fire.

Charlie Company

There wasn't much time to stop and think about what had transpired over the last few days. Patrols were still being sent out and new orders were trickling down from the battalion level. The battlefield evolved by the hour. The company waited until late in the night hours to begin the transition to a new CP, moving about 500 meters east of their location. The Charlie Company Marines were ordered to set up in an old school house. They scrambled to gather their gear, weapons, ammo, and rockets. The darkness magnified the confusion. Moving over a hundred Marines from point A to point B was not a special operation. It was no secret when and where they were going. The enemy was likely inundated with smashing footsteps, like a rumble of elephants passing by. By this time, the Marines were somewhat desensitized to the danger. Stealth was compromised, to say the least, by clumsy feet and oversized packs. The most common term used to describe those situations is a "gaggle-fuck," which is when a group of Marines intend on doing things the way the "plan" describes, but things evolve into something less-sophisticated and grossly more unorganized than one would hope.

One after another, in single file, they moved along the road with large silhouetted, mansions looming overhead. It an upscale neighborhood, containing elaborately built houses with high walls and gates. Walking into the school house, the Marines first noticed the roof had collapsed. There were desks, chairs, and debris everywhere from US air strikes. The "gaggle fuck" quickly turned into a "cluster-fuck" as the Marines bottled up in the entrance, trying to coordinate living space, and maintain platoon integrity. They began arguing and bickering over this and that. It's one of the more poignant realities of infantry life. The Officers, with all their "god-like powers" were responsible for large-scale company movements and the logistical support that comes with that. Although, when it didn't go as planned, they virtually always blamed the NCOs.

From day one, a Marine is taught to "shut the fuck up, do what you are told, and follow the guy in front of you!" And then, when that happens and no one has a clue as to what is going on, they ask why nobody took the initiative to unfuck the situation. The opposite of this is having too many chefs in the kitchen. In other words, there were often too many egos vying for solutions and not enough minions to accomplish the tasks. It was a vicious cycle. Realizing that the schoolhouse was not big enough to accommodate the entire company, Captain Quiet gave the order to separate the Marines by platoons into two separate buildings on the corner of a neighborhood, adjacent to the large field in front of the schoolhouse.

Second Platoon and their Weapons Platoon attachments cleared and occupied a house to the West of the field and First and Third Platoons, with their attachments, occupied the building to the East. Second Platoon enjoyed better accommodations, since their residence was painted, decorated, and somewhat furnished. First and Third set up in a huge three story house, but half-finished with mere plaster and concrete framing. The windows were open, rebar jutted from the walls, and debris was scattered about. They quickly designated space between the squads and repeated the ritual - unpack gear, clean weapons, make a list of something, acquire and eat chow, drink water, check ammo, pass brevity codes, challenges and passwords, make a fire watch list, make a gear list, fight over a porn magazine, talk shit, shave, take a shit, brush teeth, et cetera, but not necessarily in that order. Day turned into night and everything became quiet. Talking turned to whispers and laughing to giggles. Some Marines had already seized the opportunity to get some sleep if they had no immediate duties to conclude. D-Day plus 4 had ended.

Chapter 4
Lucky 13

November 13, 2004 - First Platoon, Charlie Company

The next day, the Command ordered First Platoon to clear a block of houses surrounding the new patrol base Charlie Company had set up the day before. First Platoon consisted of only two squads of 13 Marines each, which was small. Most platoons consisted of three squads of 12 or more. Charlie Company geared up and departed on their next mission just as the sun breached the horizon. The air was chilly. The plan was to envelope the squads to the West, systematically clear each house on the block, and head back to the East toward their patrol base.

The AmTracs joined in support, which was advantageous because they possessed up-armored mounts with heavy guns, like the M2 .50 caliber machine gun and a MK-19 automatic grenade launcher. The houses were all two stories or more with high walls and annexes of space on the sides. By then, Charlie Company learned to engage target buildings with a method of "prepping" or going in "hot." In other words, they would fire a rocket into the top level of the house to flush out any potential enemy before Marines ever entered.

Later, Command would stress going in "cold" (no prepping fire) when collateral damage became a political issue. Ideally, they wanted to enter each house from top to bottom. However, this tactic wasn't always possible and it is extremely difficult to scale high walls without ladders. Inevitably, there were many times when they were forced to enter from bottom to top, making stairways and doorways prime kill zones. Once the Marines entered a house to clear it, there needed to be a high level of commitment, because if a fight ensued within the house, the chance of high casualties was inevitable. If they could expose the enemy before making that commitment, they could just cordon off the area and lay waste to everything. But, that required a "positive ID." Most often, the only way to get positive ID was to meet the enemy face to face.

Essentially, the Marines would allow the enemy to ambush them, so they could get an exact fix on their position and destroy them afterwards. None of the Marines from the highest ranks to the lowest had ever been taught this tactic! When and where the Marines would meet the enemy was almost always dictated by the enemy, unless the Marines happened to catch them in the open. As such, the insurgents would essentially pick and choose when they would make jihad and die. Simply put, when they engaged the Marines, they usually died. Escape was futile, as the Marines steadily weeded them out. It became more and more challenging for them to move, let alone acquire ammo, supplies, and weapons. The assault men fired a few "spotting rounds" into the target area. This tactic was apparently taught in the training manual, but did not serve conducive to actual combat operations because it alerted the enemy to the Marines' presence and location. Furthermore, the tactic took too long and sapped the momentum of charging into a house from the bottom up.

Through trial and error, Charlie Company became savvy to the limitations of doctrine, and began placing well-aimed rockets into windows and doorways. Large iron gates were bound up with chains and big locks. Many of the wealthier homeowners attempted to lock up and secure their houses from the fighting. As such, almost every lock needed to be blown off and every door kicked in. Those were the orders and Marines didn't question orders (sarcasm). Napoleon and his assault section continued blowing each gate with C-4 and sending rockets into the house to prep, "BOOM, BOOM!" After First and Second Squads of First Platoon had cleared the first six houses of the block and were moving in the direction of their CP. The searches yielded no sign of the enemy.

They came up on a large and menacing structure. It was dark and devoid of decor. Weed, Cowboy, and Groucho from Second Squad entered the house and immediately came out saying it smelled like gas everywhere. They bounded to another doorway, around the wall anticipating there would be an alternate entrance. Unbeknownst to them, the entrance they found led to a completely separate house in a confusing maze of stone walls. Then, First Squad came up from behind them and entered the same smelly house that Second Squad had just exited. The two squads became separated in adjacent houses. Fish was the First Squad Leader of First Platoon. A minister's son, Fish was an amicable and trusted Marine.

He stacked up behind his point man, Malik. Harley stood ready in the middle, then Blade with the SAW in the rear. The two squads entered each house simultaneously. Facing toward the South, Fish's squad was on the right and Moke's squad was on the left. Second Platoon stood over watch, across the street, on the roof of their CP. Weapons and elements of Third Platoon were to the East of their position covering the left flank with M240G medium machine-guns. Upon First Squad's entry, Malik scanned and cleared the bottom deck with Harley. The rest of the squad followed in trace. They passed a stairwell and a room to the left. Suddenly, Cherokee noticed an insurgent pop out from the top of the stairwell with an AK-47, firing at them. "OH SHIT," they screamed!

Automatic gunfire began ripping through the ceiling and the Marines returned fire, killing the insurgent. He slumped over and slid down the stairway. Malik rushed forward to a room to find cover, as Beef followed closely. Shadows passed from slits in the walls, providing an obstructed view of an alleyway behind the house. Harley unloaded a magazine through his M-16. Red tracers penetrated the walls and screams filled the room as the insurgents dropped down several grenades from mouse holes in the ceiling. The desperate struggle to gain a foothold was costly. The room filled with smoke from exploded grenades. The Marines tried to gather their bearing, but the gunfire was so deafening and intense that nobody could hear or communicate.

Two more grenades dropped from the ceiling and the Marines scrambled to hug the walls. Harley is hit and pushed down with a forceful blast. His back became warm and wet. He pushed open a door to the bathroom and then closed it, moving out to a back alley full of scrap metal and bordered by a high wall. It looked like a bad idea. More grenades dropped from above, "BOOM, BOOM!!" One of the explosions hit Harley with the force of a sledgehammer. He dragged himself toward the doorway, where they had entered. Several Marines were hit and bleeding, leaning against the wall, and others were being dragged outside. Doc B intently focused on treating the others despite taking shrapnel in his leg and back. Blade lost a finger, Razor had shrapnel in his eye, Georgia was shot in the foot, and Bull and Skinny were riddled with hot metal all over. Fish was pinned down against the curb on the other side of the street as he sheltered the body of a wounded and screaming Marine, amidst the gunfire and grenade play.

The AmTracs pulled up immediately and provided security on the block during the clearing operations that day. Cherokee, Fish, and some of the others squad members helped to drag the Marines around a wall to the curb of the street, as the AmTracs pulled up. The incessant gunfire and concussive explosions from grenade and rockets from both sides impeded the evacuation. The ten wounded Marines from first squad crawled and dragged themselves and each other from the ambush house. At the same time, the insurgents upstairs ran around on the second and third decks of the fortified structure. This offered ample targets for the Marines in the over watch position across the street. The aforementioned tragedy became something of a turkey shoot. A ferocious fight raged directly above their heads and the chaotic MedEvac of the wounded slowly progressed. They brought the extent of their assets to bear on the house with heavy machine guns and anti-armor rockets.

Sandman positioned himself on the roof with Second Platoon's over watch. "Gimme that goddamn rocket, Devil Dawg," he shouted to a junior Marine. Aiming from his shoulder in a standing position, Sandman fired the AT-4 into the third deck of the house. The rocket exploded, turning one of the retreating insurgents into a "pink mist." A pink mist refers to when an explosion literally causes the human body to virtually disintegrate into a million pieces of bone and flesh – a mist. Initially, nobody charged stairwells in a full frontal counter-attack. The Marines focused on defending their positions and treating the wounded. The mission immediately turned from "sweep and clear" to "extract and MedEvac." The over watch position continued pounding the ambush house. The enemy was exposed and paid the ultimate price for fighting them. Meanwhile, Second Squad was pinned down from the merciless gunfire in the adjacent house, mostly from friendly forces in the over watch. The intensity of the engagement sent shards of metal and a barrage of flying lead everywhere.

The Marines began to clear the first deck of the separate side of the house. As they moved up the stairway to a door leading to the roof, the melee re-ignited. They looked out of the only exit to the street as bullets whizzed and chipped into the walls. The barrage of friendly machine guns and secondary explosions rained down on their position. At the time, they were not sure what was actually happening. They didn't know the situation of First Squad. They couldn't hear anything except the deafening battlefield chaos, and there was no communication on the handheld radio. Several requests for a SitRep were unfulfilled. They all pointed their weapons outboard, anticipating that the insurgents would get flushed out to their flank, and down the alleyways. Shadows passed the exposed cracks of light in the concrete, like somebody was running back and forth. It lasted for several minutes, but seemed like an eternity as time seemed to pass in slow motion.

Finally, a relay message came through on the walkie-talkie. "We're pinned down over here, you have to get out on your own," exclaimed Country. Moments later, Moke pressed for the squad to make a hasty exit and fall back to the firm base to regroup. He patted himself down for a yellow smoke grenade and yelled, "'Fuck, I just had one, where is it?" JD reached down into his pouch and pulled one out. "Brilliant! Just shoot it into the street." The U.S. military teaches that popping yellow smoke is a designated signal for friendly forces to shift their fire, so as to allow friendly units to maneuver from a position.

Meanwhile, First Squad had loaded their wounded on the AmTracs, and departed to Bravo Surgical triage center at Camp Fallujah, a few miles outside the city. Fish, Cherokee, and Bean Stalk had already returned to the firm base, and Doc C was applying bandages to Cherokee for some minor shrapnel wounds. Second Squad popped the smoke as the over watch gun position on the left flank adjusted to allow them an opportunity to move. Filing out into the street, they bounded back to join the rest of the platoon.

Through all the commotion, the remaining superficially wounded and able-bodied members of First Squad returned to the company CP. During the initial entry of the house when the ambush began, Malik, the point man, and Beef, a rifleman, remained hunkered down in the room that they defended during the firefight. They couldn't hear the other Marines, and dare not shout out to them. It was eerily quiet for a few tense moments, unknowing that their squad mates had pulled out of the house. They sat silent, looking at each other from the back corners of the room, making hand gestures for a hasty exit. Suddenly, they could hear Arabic chatter from above. The enemy fighters were still jostling around on the second deck in the brief cease in gunfire.

Malik realized they would have to expose themselves again and dash past the stairway in order to escape the house. Beef and Malik looked at each other, making hand gestures, and then focused back on the doorway, where their muzzles were intently fixed. "Allah Akbar...Allah Akbar!!" Footsteps ran down the stairs with an assertive rumble. Donned with various weapons, gear, and ammunition, a fire team of insurgents followed each other in a single file sprint, making the pivot from the stairs into the room to their right. Immediately, the enemy faced a hail of bullets from Malik and Beef, who were knelt in a firing position from opposite corners of the room with their M-16s. Furiously pulling back on the triggers in semi-automatic mode, the insurgents fell to the floor. One by one, all three slightly stacked upon the other like dominos. Their inertia while entering the room in force propelled their already lifeless bodies forward. Being met with such a staunch defensive posture, the enemy was literally stopped "dead in their tracks," falling to the deck in front of the Marines' feet.

Only the two Marines who defended the room had witnessed the remarkable spectacle. Pumping a few more rounds into their bodies, as the stillness of death was confirmed. After a few intense seconds, they rose to their feet and listened for more movement. There would be no better time to exit. They broke out, moving intently from the bedroom, into the living room, and back out the doorway to the street. They linked back up with the rest of the platoon at the CP. Still processing what had just taken place, Beef and Malik joined what was left of First Platoon. Beef was a jovial personality by nature. However, when the others approached to ask what had happened to them, he just looked stoically into their faces and said, "You have no idea what these eyes have seen!"

November 13, 2004 Alpha Company Third Platoon

As platoons from Charlie Company fiercely repelled an ambush, a few blocks to the West, Alpha Company also cleared houses. First and Third Squads from Third Platoon, Alpha Company were ordered to clear a block of 15 houses. The two squads split up the block and cleared the houses from opposite directions and meet in the middle. This tactic would prevent the enemy from escaping to the rear. It didn't seem like a good idea to separate the squads, but it seemed necessary for containment purposes. Otherwise, the enemy could merely retreat and circle back around to the same houses the Marines had just cleared.

As the sun shined in the high noon sky, the Marines were fatigued and sweaty. They took quick breaks in between clearing each house to re-hydrate or throw down some chow. Speedy was on point. A Mexican national, he joined the Marines with only a green card and a slew of hard knock experiences. He was already a seasoned infantryman near the end of his first enlistment. The teams within the squad split off to search other parts of the house where they had stopped. They found a random AK-47 with rounds in the magazine. They requested permission from higher to use it, and then advised them not to be alarmed by the friendly fire.

None of them had ever fired an AK-47, so they welcomed any chance to do so. "POP, POP, POP," as the Marines took turns shooting the enemy's weapon.

Meanwhile, the other half of the clearing squad had meandered around to the other house to continue clearing without informing the rest of the squad. Tiny served as point man for Second Team. His name was a purposeful oxymoron because he stood nearly 6'5" in height, and offered a large silhouette. As the Marines tested the AK-47, a loud and intense volume of fire erupted from the adjacent house to the left. Unbeknownst to half of them, a Marine from another fire team in the squad kicked in a door and insurgents instantly greeted him with a barrage of automatic fire, missing him several times, as he fell back. Tiny was directly behind him and was hit three times in his armored vest and once in the helmet. Only later did he notice the nine other holes through his uniform and gear.

It was a miracle that Tiny did not even suffer a scratch. He was temporarily knocked out from the force of the bullet hitting his helmet. He fell to the ground and the Marines behind him opened up with return fire into the room, mere feet from the enemy. On the balcony above them, four more insurgents appeared firing AK-47s, an RPG, and throwing down a hail of grenades on the Marines. Speedy jumped up and saw one of them shoot an RPG toward the entrance of the house, but the rocket slammed into a wall, narrowly missing the Marines. Speedy raised his rifle and shot the enemy in the chest, putting him down for good. The intensity of the fight increased rapidly, as other insurgents revealed themselves. The Marines dug in for cover.

Two other Marines attempted to reinforce the others and make entry into the house, when another enemy shot down on them from the balcony, wounding them in the arm and legs. The squad was pinned down. Speedy was on the corner of a wall, when a wounded Marine extended his arm for help. Speedy switched his rifle to his left hand and grabbed his hand and dragged him out of the house. When they got outside, they found the others pinned down on against a wall. The remaining insurgents on the balcony continued shooting and throwing grenades down on them. Everyone was spread out in different rooms in the house. Some were hunkered down covering the Doc as he was treating the other wounded, but they had all found cover inside the house. Speedy was still outside against a wall, trading fire back and forth with the enemy. He was getting frustrated because he knew he had hit them several times already, but they stubbornly wouldn't go down. It seemed to the Marines as though the insurgents were super-human.

At the time, few Marines had learned that many insurgents ingested methamphetamines before fighting. In retrospect, it makes sense they would need to be high to pick a fight with Marine gunfighters. Having unloaded and reloaded several magazines at this point, Speedy continued to engage and the enemy tossed more grenades. He leaned away as they exploded right next to him, but miraculously the shrapnel merely grazed his arm. Speedy finally returned a grenade over the balcony wall, silencing his menacing foe. Unbeknownst to him, Speedy had been shot in his armored vest in addition to the shrapnel in his arm. Meanwhile, the remaining insurgents scrambled as Third Squad assaulted the roof of the house, finishing off the rest of the enemy fighters as they fled from their rooftop positions.

During the day's fighting, Alpha Company killed five insurgents, but several Marines sustained wounds from grenades. Alpha Company fortunately did not suffer any KIAs. Rightfully so, Tiny became a legend after the enemy shot him twelve times – once in the helmet – but remained physically unscathed. Both Speedy and Tiny refused MedEvac and carried on with their respective units into the weeks ahead. Notwithstanding Alpha Company's luck, twenty Lava Dawgs from 1/3 suffered wounds in action across the city that day. To say the least, all of them felt very grateful to be alive. Later that night, after-action reports of the day's fighting revealed the insurgent strategy. Charlie Company Marines learned a great deal about their foe, up close and personal. They now understood the enemy's tendencies and appreciated their willingness to fight to the death.

This jihadist, suicide-style, ambush was a common tactic used by the Mujahadeen. The enemy's ability to dictate the terms of when and where to engage them unnerved the Marines. Despite resulting in a low kill rate on the Marines, these building-based ambushes became their only practical method to inflict any considerable damage on the quickly advancing Marines. Furthermore, this tactic usually provided the enemy "martyrdom," which they so desperately sought. In short, their fight was futile, and they knew it. Many suffered an extremely violent death. The lucky ones had time to scream "Allah" just before meeting their maker. As far as the Marines are concerned, this final plea to some deity offered them no protection or sanctity. They survived unsupplied and starving in squalor. They constantly ran, hid, and ran some more. In hindsight, perhaps they did embrace death – but many people probably would in the same situation. By the end of the first week, the remaining enemy simply prolonged the agony of their demise.

That night, the fire watch and members of Weapons Platoon provided security on the roof. They scanned the skyline with their NVGs (Night-Vision Goggles) to keep a watchful eye and ear on the perimeter. An assertive November chill set in with a brisk breeze. The low temperature began to drop nightly. The Marines seemed to hear the most acute sounds in the silent stillness. Their ears muffled the wind. The Marines felt no emotion if not the desire to kill the rest of those motherfuckers. But, the darkness limits one's ability to fight at night, regardless of the technology he wields.

Eventually, the Charlie Company Marines became paranoid. Turbo, Guns, and Napoleon muttered some words amongst themselves. "Do you guys hear that", asked Turbo. Napoleon stood up, peeking his head over the wall, looking down to the street. "I think it's coming from that house across the street," he replied. The sound continued for almost an hour. "Man, it sounds like someone is trying to hammer through a wall", Turbo complained.

By this time, they had become savvy to the insurgents. The Marines now understood how the enemy tunneled mouse holes between structures to gain escape routes when their position became compromised. This eliminated the need to venture on the street or jump between rooftops, exposing themselves to vengeful Marines. The "cats" hunted and the "mice" evaded and attempted to steal the night. It proved an ingenious method to counter the superior US forces. While sporadic firefights would unfold in the darkness across the city, the Marines grew frustrated as Command restricted the ROEs. The day's casualties rattled Captain Quiet. As a result, he began ordering the Marines to acquire "positive ID" before engaging a target, but it was, and is, nearly impossible to "positively ID" anything in the dark, even with NVGs. The insurgents used the night to move and reposition themselves. They appeared disciplined in that way.

They watched the Marines, and tried to move in close, under the cover of darkness. Napoleon was a short, stocky Chicagoan. He had some urban grit to his character, but everybody felt the same way he did. He didn't want to wait around to get hit. He wanted to relentlessly stomp all signs of threats until nothing stood. After all, this is what they had been taught. After a while, it seemed some officer at some level would order the Marines to pull back, or outright deny requests to engage, at the risk of "collateral damage." At the end of the day, their lives were measured in that respect. Instead, Marines were traded for conserving people's homes – the same homes that aided and abetted the insurgency and provided a platform for them to gain strength and control the city of Fallujah.

The Marine Corps trained enlisted grunts to destroy without pretense, but trained the officers to be gentlemen. The relationship resembled that of a dog and his master. The dog tirelessly tugged on the leash, salivating at the mouth, and the master pulled him back, denying him his savage liberties. However, when the right opportunity arose, the dog lashed out and chased whatever moved.

After Command busted Napoleon down to PFC (Private First Class), he couldn't make many decisions, but he could convince others to see his way. Regardless of rank, the assault and demolition Marines respected him. Napoleon walked down to the second deck, as Moke and Wildo lied there on their packs, bullshitting near a chemlight. Napoleon explained, "Hey guys, we keep hearing all kinds of noise across the street, like digging or chiseling. I know these fuckers are plotting some shit on us. I wanna fire a fuckin' rocket in that shit, man!" Moke's eyes lit up as he locked eyes with Wildo. "Well, let's just do it then," responded Moke. "Yeah, but the command is stressing "positive ID," interjected Wildo. Moke immediately replied, "Fuck that! I ain't waitin' for these motherfuckers to kill me.

You saw what happened to Fish's squad today? That could've been, maybe should've been, us! I ain't waiting for them to get close enough to hit us again." They coordinated the plan and synchronized their watches.

Moke and the others walked down the lines, whispering to the men, telling them to "saddle up" for a hasty ambush in a few minutes. Gunner was just chilling next to the M240G machine gun, sipping on an Arabic labeled, Mountain Dew. They felt elated to expend some rounds at night. When they fired military tracer ammo at night, the tracers and explosions emitted a glorious light show.

At 2105 hours, they initiated the attack with a single rocket shot. The SMAW launched its projectile into the window of the target house. The detonation created a massive vacuum of pressure that sucked in the air and spit it back out, exploding a fireball of concrete and debris. The entire company joined the attack with a ferocious volume of fire from the rooftops and windowsills. A symphony of SAWs fired at the cyclic rate, expending countless rounds, while rifle magazines were emptied and reloaded. The tremendous gunfire engulfed the scene for several minutes.

Only the width of the street below separated the Marines from their target – virtually point blank given their skills. At this range, the sheer volume of fire on the house ignited the structure into flames well into the night, rendering it uninhabitable for the remaining enemy. Merc expended two drums of ammo from his SAW. He hadn't changed the barrel, and it was white hot, nearly translucent. Pepe filmed the spectacular display of prowess with his helmet cam.

After several minutes a Staff Sergeant yelled, "Cease fire, Cease fire! What the fuck is going on?" Everyone, but he, laughed. One Marine responded, "Someone started shootin', so we all started shootin'." "What! Pass it up the chain, GODDAMMIT!", countered the Staff Sergeant harshly. But, the average grunt viewed their proactive approach to urban warfare as beneficial, for they now understood their advantage declined with their momentum. In football terms, they wanted their offense to stay on the battlefield to give their defense time to rest. Doctrine reinforced the notion of unleashing overwhelming firepower at every possible opportunity, especially when the momentum favored them. Marine grunts became famous for this persistently violent nature.

They did not aim for "one shot, one kill," to which snipers aspire. They aspired and intended to over kill from the moment they arrived in country. They had been crated like dogs for far too long. They all understood this, but Command expected an answer for every engagement. They needed to provide an "after-action report." Command usually kept tabs on everything, yet never had an answer for anything. A popular catch-phrase trickled through the companies: "What the fuck you gonna do to me, send me to Fallujah?"

The sentiments went viral throughout the enlisted ranks, the guys who were thrown directly into the fray each day. Most guys knew they would only commit to a 4-year stint on the military and get out. "Who did it? Who the fuck started it," the Staff Sergeant demanded from the unit leaders. "Uh ... I don't know Staff Sergeant, everybody just started shooting," The whole company laughed and conversed amongst each other in a low roar. They were loyal to the underground. They would never drop a dime on another Marine for risking his ass to benefit the unit, regardless of whether or not anyone occupied the target house. After losing almost half a platoon that day, the Charlie Marines were jumpy, paranoid, and vengeful. The interior of the surrounding structures burned throughout the night, providing the Marines some light with which to observe the area with some solace.

Chapter 5
East Manhattan

November 14, 2004 Charlie Company Second Platoon

The previous day's engagement crippled First Platoon, which later consisted of one fire team and a squad. Capt. Quiet ordered Second Platoon to re-enter the ambush house the next morning to get a BDA (Battle Damage Assessment). The houses to the East of the target still burned from the previous night's assault. The AmTracs approached the large embattled structure and Second Platoon climbed from the tops of AmTracs to reach the second deck of the house. They expected they might encounter resistance, so they were pleasantly surprised when they did not. Upon entering the rooms, however, the sweetly pungent odor of death hit them immediately. Several bodies decomposed on the floor – black and bloated. They were riddled with bullets, shrapnel. Most were covered by broken concrete. Some had no visible faces.

The Marines found three corpses on the bottom deck, where First Squad had been hit. They were virtually piled on top of one another in the side room, confirming Malik and Beef's account of gunning them down in extremely close quarters. Altogether, they counted sixteen bodies, including three on the roof, and two more outside in the alleyways. One still grasped onto life, as he slowly and painfully crawled out of a back door. Smiley stood over him, observing curiously, before he ended the enemy's misery. His skull popped open from the pressure like a coconut, oozing brain matter from underneath. The Marines were surprised to learn many of the insurgents were not from Iraq, but rather were Mujahadeen, Muslim foreign fighters from Yemen, Saudi Arabia, Syria, Chechnya, and Kuwait. They had strategically positioned nearly 100 RPGs, PKM medium-machine guns, and AK-47s throughout the house. Thousands of rounds of ammunition, hundreds of rockets, and grenades were strewn about. All of them had suitcases stashed, wearing two to three layers of clothing. They had cell phones, GPS, passports, and thousands in 50 and 100-dollar bills of US currency. Second Platoon collected the remaining intelligence and tended to the ghastly task of pulling the dead from the rubble and piling their bodies out near the street.

Askari District

The Battalion Commander, Mad Mike, ordered 1/3 to halt their advance north of MSR Fran, and begin re-clearing the affluent neighborhoods in a large swath of the northeastern part of the city known to Fallujans as the Askari District. US Forces codenamed it "East Manhattan." Fallujah was known as a favored vacation spot for Sunni businessman, Baath Party members, and the high command of Saddam's former army. Owning a seasonal home in the Askari section of Fallujah reflected the scale of Iraqi opulence often associated with the wealthy and powerful.

The Askari streets boasted enormous mansions, two to three stories high, immaculately plastered and painted to deflect the powerful rays of the Iraqi sun. They featured impressive landscaping with freshly green sprouts of grass and flowered ornamental bushes, gardens of hanging vines, and pottery fixtures, indicative of the ancient remnants of Babylon. There were multiple carports, meticulously-laid sidewalks of brick, stone, and mortar. Some residents even left their Mercedes behind in the driveway. Ten-foot walls and ironclad gates surrounded these relative palaces, as stone pillars graced their entrances. Stained-glass windows highlighted the bathrooms, which were all fitted with flushing toilets, and bidets. The Marines found it odd to see these so-called mud-hut dwellers living so extravagantly. A few blocks to the East and South, the houses were half constructed frames and dilapidated shanties of an entirely different class and sort. Nonetheless, Askari served as an important hub of activity and intelligence gathering, given its strategic egress routes for the insurgency. These were the homes of powerful men with loyalty to the old regime. Askari provided a level of influence that could facilitate resistance. By no coincidence, it provided the stage for some of the bloodiest fighting in the Fallujah – the "City of Mosques."

Early that morning, Sgt. Peralta volunteered to stack up with one of the squads during more of the daily clearing operations, because the squad had taken many casualties. As a Platoon Guide, he served an advisor role. He did not need to be involved with assaults and kicking in doors. The young twenty-somethings would do that, the PFCs, Lance Corporals, and Corporals who put their lives on the line every time they entered a house. Everyone has a job description according to rank and billet. Often, Sergeants and higher did not clear houses or were required be directly on the front lines, especially in an urban environment. In urban scenarios, the higher-ups served a logistics and command role, as opposed to focusing narrowly on any one particular assault. With that said, senior NCOs (Non-Commissioned Officers), SNCOs (Staff NCOs) and Officers who willingly charged into firefights were much more revered and inspirational, in the eyes of their Marines.

However, Peralta was different from the sort. He was quiet but bullheaded. Undaunted, he stubbornly insisted on being there in the thick of things. He expatriated from Mexico and was the head of his family since his father died. He wanted to fight for his citizenship and earn a better life for his mother and siblings with his sacrifice. After clearing a few houses on the block, they entered the fourth house of the day.

Peralta pushed open the door to a first-level room in order to begin clearing. Immediately, he was riddled in the chest by a burst of AK-47 fire and he fell forward. The Marines directly behind him fell back, startled. They regrouped on the wall from a better angle and an insurgent tossed a grenade toward them, landing close to Peralta. Everyone hugged the walls and braced for the explosion. Mortally wounded, Peralta reached out, grabbed the grenade, and heroically tucked it under his chest before it exploded. With his rare and selfless act, he saved the lives of the rest of the Marines in the house. The Marines later re-assaulted the house, killing three insurgents and retrieving Peralta's body.

Peralta was nominated for the Congressional Medal of Honor, America's highest military award for valor in combat. After refusing to accept a lesser award, the Navy Cross, Peralta's family still awaits the results of a new nomination for the highest award. Two separate Secretaries of Defense have declined to confirm his nomination. The Secretaries, which are ultimately the last line of approval before the President signs a nomination, cited a discrepancy in the forensic evidence.

KIA – November 15, 2004
Sgt. Rafael Peralta, 25, Mexico City, Mexico

After a week, the initial assault was wrapping up. The four Marine Infantry Battalions held their positions. The city was divided up and each battalion controlled a specific AO. Battalion 1/3 was tasked with the Northeastern section – the Askari District, where all of their enemy engagements had occurred in the recent days. Their AO ran from East to West, from the Clover Leaf to PL ("Phase Line") Ethan, and north to south from ASR ("Alternate Supply Route") Golden to MSR ("Main Supply Route") Michigan. The Battalion designated which blocks each company would clear, house-to-house, room-to-room, for more days to come.

November 16, 2004 - Humanitarian Effort

The Brass moved forward with Phase 4 of their plan, which consisted of allowing civilians back into the city, assessing the damage to their homes, and trying to return to some semblance of normalcy. After one week of intense house-to-house combat, Command declared that offensive combat operations in Fallujah were finished. Of course, this wasn't the case, but in terms of political success and placating the international media, prolonging the idea that the city was "not yet secure" seemed impractical. The job for the Marines would grow even tougher as Command further restricted the ROEs. Trying to discern between civilian and combatant served nearly impossible, until it was too late. Attempting to deliver aid where needed further complicated a dangerous scenario.

Many of the people came back to their homes only to find them demolished. They had no job, food, water, or sanitation. Some salvaged generators or kerosene lamps for light and electricity. Few were delighted that their homes remained intact, and seemed to gesture approval of the Marines being there. The Marines were conditioned to be able to transition from delivering a relentless offensive onslaught to caring for wounded civilians and issuing rations. That intrinsic dichotomy is what separates Marines from absolute barbarians. On the battlefield, they did what they needed to make it home – nothing more, nothing less. Marines earned the nickname "Devil Dogs" because they are capable of simultaneously being remarkably loyal and ferocious. This is the professional standard by which the Marines approached their duty.

November 18, 2004 -The Red Crescent

Command ordered First Platoon to patrol over to Second Platoon's position at the Red Crescent Hospital, the Islamic version of the Red Cross. They had been engaged in a firefight that morning, taking small arms fire from nearby buildings. US forces had received information indicating insurgents routinely used Red Crescent ambulances to transport weapons and wounded fighters. While Second Platoon was clearing and chasing down the perpetrators, First Platoon secured the hospital. There was evidence inside to suggest that they were treating wounded insurgents. Bloody bandages, syringes, and tools for surgery were scattered about. It was a large complex with multiple levels. The Marines ascended to the roof in support of the adjacent platoon. Fashioned to a broomstick was an Iraqi Flag, bearing the Arabic inscription of Saddam's former regime. One of the Marines tore it down and balled it up in his cargo pocket as a souvenir – another unexpected opportunity to score a battlefield souvenir.

Down on the street, the buzz was going around about a hot blonde news reporter who was milling around their position. Any female was a welcomed sight. Her attributes were inflated to a much higher degree, due to their sheer deprivation of encounters with the opposite sex. She was tough and hearty. Most of them couldn't imagine why she wanted to be there. Decked out with a kevlar helmet and armored vest, she was hungry for a story. Some were eager to offer up some info and be interviewed, maybe get their photo taken and printed across every newspaper in the Free World. "Wouldn't that be somethin'! My beautiful mug plastered on the front page of my hometown paper," said Cowboy. "Yeah, Lebanon, Tennessee, population 8", Weed chuckled. "You'd be a real celebrity."

Soup and Rasta's squads had rounded up six suspected insurgents during their clearing of the block. They escorted them down the street and handed them over to First Platoon to process them as EPWs (Enemy Prisoner of War) and transport them to Abu Ghraib prison for questioning. The Marines felt positive these particular EPWs were the men, who were involved in the ambush attack on them earlier in the day. Many of them dressed cleanly and wearing sandals, claiming to be university students. A few were scared, but the others remained defiantly oblivious to the Marine attempts at gathering information from them. At that point, it grew harder to differentiate between good guys and bad guys, because after opening the city, there were several people loitering on random corners, staring with hate filled eyes.

Now, unless otherwise involved in a hostile act, the locals were free to wander during the day. They were perfectly positioned to make key observations for the insurgency, spending the daylight hours before curfew taking intricate notes about the Marines, like size, equipment, etc. This information was very valuable to the insurgents. The Marines wanted to just kill them on site, but harsh penalties would be enforced for war crimes, including courts martial. With all the camera crews running around, the Marines were tight-lipped and well aware of a potential media backlash.

"Here you go man, these guys are yours now. But watch out for this guy, he's Poopy Pants," said Soup with an exaggerated laugh. He put a finger under his nose, grimacing. "Look," as he pointed to one of the suspects. They were all on their knees, legs crossed, and hands bound behind their back, leaning against the wall with their head. It was an uncomfortable position and they would remain that way for several hours until a Humvee arrived to pick them up later that evening. Moke looked over at Poopy Pants. The guy had defecated himself. It smelled rancid, and to make it worse, a massive colony of flies had congregated on his backside, swarming around a smorgasbord of fecal matter fermenting in his underwear. They took turns kicking him and baiting him for a reaction. Each time the flies would get startled, dissipate in the air, and then land again in the same spot around his ass.

The Marines were ridiculing him and laughing hysterically. Making up little rhymes like, "Come on Poopy Pants, do your dance ... come on Poopy Pants, it's your last chance!" Some of the detainees muttered broken English denouncing Saddam, begging for a pardon. Others mumbled prayers to Allah, but Poopy Pants remained stubborn in his humiliation, embracing it. This is when the harsh reality of war emerges. They were human beings, albeit the enemy. After all, both sides killed each other, inflicted merciless pain, and tormented the other. Then, a brief thought of humanity and compassion is quickly overshadowed by the reality that ten minutes ago, these captives were shooting to kill them.

They moved Poopy Pants to a back room because he was trying to communicate with the others. The squad leader relieved the young Lance Corporal who was guarding him. "Hey Doc, lemme see your M9. Take a break, Shooter," he ordered. Poopy Pants was visibly more exhausted than before. Kneeling for hours, the blood flow to his extremities had slowly constricted, so his extremities became numb. The Marine cocked back his pistol, placing a round in the chamber. He then ejected it, just before putting the weapon to the insurgent's temple and pulling the trigger. Poopy Pants flinched at the sound of the hammer engaging. He repeated this act over and over for several minutes. He wanted to shoot him in the head. But at the same time, he felt pity for him. If by some chance he wasn't already a hardcore insurgent, with the ensuing weeks of processing and questioning at Abu Ghraib Prison, would surely motivate him to become one out of sheer vengeance. In the end, it was all relative. Everyone was guilty, because they had no choice but to be guilty. After succumbing to the reality of a lifetime at Leavenworth Prison, the Marine regrouped and quietly exited the room.

Command ordered First Platoon to keep watch over the detainees until the transport unit picked him up. They were to hold in place for the night, and launch another patrol in the morning. Meanwhile, the guys were hungry and bored with eating MREs. They could hear chickens squabbling over the wall in the next house. Weed climbed over the wall to have a look and noticed two small malnourished chickens in a wire cage. The rest of his team followed in trace. They cleared the bottom level of the house, and kitchen area, scouring for anything edible or to use for cooking. They managed to acquire a pot and a propane tank. Cowboy entered the cage with Weed trying to collect the evasive squawking chickens. The chickens yelped and let out blood-curdling screams. Weed quickly grabbed the chickens by the neck and began hurling their bodies in a circular motion, breaking their necks. Some of the city slickers of the group just witnessed the situation, befuddled. "Ya'll see, it's that easy," exclaimed Weed, as he spit out a wad of Copenhagen.

Just an everyday thing he had done a hundred times before, back on the ranch in Idaho. Minutes later, the nerves of the chicken still produced a jolting muscular reflex. "Well, who wants to skin em'? I got my trusty K-Bar over here." Weed pulled it out, admiring the sharpened blade. Moke looked over, "Give it here, I'll do it. I might have to skin a chicken someday, might as well learn it now." Weed instructed him how to first cut off the head and feet, and Moke started the meticulous process of gutting, skinning, and de-feathering the animal, careful not to release the bile sac. After both of the chickens were cleaned, the group seemed unimpressed with the size of the edible portion of the poultry. Nonetheless, the birds provided each member of the squad an equally proportionate morsel. Fashioning together the propane tank to the burner required some MacGyver-like skills, but it was nothing a Gerber or Leatherman couldn't fix. Gerber and Leatherman tools provided an amazing array of tools assembled neatly together in a convenient small, self-contained unit. They contain a plethora of gadgets that can get a creative tactician out of all kinds of jams. After 20 minutes of boiling, they pulled the chicken apart into 13 different equal pieces, enough for each man to have a taste. The bite lacked any salt or seasoning, but it was hot and delicious. This act of sharing and camaraderie galvanized the men. It provided a chance to view their predicament from a different, humble, perspective.

Combat Cameraman Klein

Combat Camera had been attached to the Black Sheep Squad since D-Day. He was sent over from Headquarters Marine Corps, in DC. There were only a few of them scattered throughout various units of the battalion. When he reported to the squad, everyone seemed skeptical of the new guy, especially a POG (Personnel Other than Grunt) with a camera. Yet, he was still a Marine, and was expected to be proficient with his rifle, along with his camera related tasks. "Every Marine is a rifleman" is the mantra. He was quiet and humble, expecting to be hazed by his grunt counterparts, or just ignored completely.

"Hey listen up gents, this is our Combat Camera Guy," instructed Moke. Groans and scoffs immediately ensued. Cowboy shouted out in a drawl, "This like some Full Metal Jacket shit! Ya seen much combat," he asked. "Yeah like any of us have," interjected Moke. "We're just a bunch of salty two pump chumps! The most combat we have seen was fucking some Filipino pussy in Angeles City!" Roaring hollers and nostalgia followed. "Hey, in all seriousness, everybody welcome Combat

Camera to the squad. He might make you famous, or he might save your life, ya never know". Turning back to him and lowering his voice, Moke asked Camera if he could handle spread loading some of the weight of ammunition and rockets. Everyone was trying to get rid of some shit. Too many flares, smoke grenades, and red star clusters. Chow, water, and ammo became a priority. But, they also had to carry supporting gear, like C4, rockets, and other essentials for the assault men, and thousands of 7.62mm linked ammo for the machine gunners. It was truly a team effort.

"Uh, sure Corporal, however I can help," responded Camera. In the days following the breach, he was a good operator and integrated well with the other Marines. He moved, followed, carried gear, accurately fired his weapon, and still found time to take photos. He proved to be a remarkable multi-tasker. He quickly learned to trust the grunts, even if they didn't trust him. He had his own job to do for the Washington, D.C. Marine Corps. For archival and intelligence gathering purposes, as well as enhanced after-action reporting, Camera would provide the Marine Corps a significant resource. Perhaps a story seems more credible when a Marine can get in close to depict what is war. It's usually not the standard for civilian reporters to get so close that they are immersed in the actual combat. However, this coveted position made being a Marine reporter truly unique.

Since cameras were invented, they were used to document various conflicts, capturing the emotion and savageness of war from a firsthand point of view. As famously depicted, "The Flag Raising on Iwo Jima" still invigorates the reputation of the Marines by inspiring support and serving as symbols of American Resolve. The grunts were impressed with Camera's abilities and that he managed to hang with them. He garnered some reverence during many tough firefights. Jokingly, they developed an affinity for him, much like that of a Navy Corpsman, and celebrated him as an "Honorary Grunt". They razzed him about his daring photographic escapades, "Hey Rafterman, Mother Green and her Killing Machine," they sang, alluding to the characters from "Full Metal Jacket."

November 22, 2004 – Alpha Company, Third Platoon

On another clearing mission, like any other day, Alpha Company conducted operations in their sector of East Manhattan. Command ordered them to continue searching another block on the map. That afternoon, for some reason, did not feel right. It was too quiet. Upon entering the house, Speedy was on point, as usual. They quickly cleared the bottom level. Speedy halted momentarily to grill one of his squad mates for not paying attention and moving lethargically. "You better get your head on a swivel, Devil Dawg," Speedy demanded. Just then, Cohen bounded in front of the stack, as they moved down the hallway, and kicked open the door to a room on the left. Cohen rushed in and an insurgent was waiting in the corner. An AK-47 burst rang out, impacting Cohen in the side of his chest, as he instantly fell, face down. Speedy was right behind him and took two rounds to the leg, shattering his femur.

The rest of the stack initially fell back from the gunfire, but quickly repositioned. They charged in and overwhelmed the insurgent with gunfire, killing him. Speedy was lying in the hallway, bleeding profusely. As he started nodding off, the Corpsman ran to his aid and dragged him outside to call for a MedEvac. After the initial bloody confrontation, the firefight ensued for a few more hours as the squads engaged with other remaining insurgents in the house. It was not until they assaulted a few more times that were they able to kill the remaining fighters and recover Cohen's body. Speedy survived his wounds, but his buddy wasn't so lucky. Cpl. Michael R. Cohen, 23, from Jacobus, PA, died from a single bullet that found its way into his lungs, in between his protective body armor. Years later, Garrett Anderson would produce "The November War," a documentary produced to depict that fateful day for Alpha Company.

After two weeks of offensive operations, the four Marine Infantry Battalions involved in Operation Phantom Fury were poised to hold key tactical positions and send out patrols from barricaded compounds known as firm bases. They were usually former schoolhouses. The Marines picked them because they were well built concrete structures with several rooms, elevated positions, and plenty of space from which to operate their vehicles. Battalion 3/5 was originally located on the western edge of Fallujah along the Euphrates River in an area known as the Jolan District. It was the oldest part of Fallujah, and thought to be the most heavily concentrated insurgent area. Battalion 3/1 was to the right of their California-based brethren, driving all the way to the southern edge of Fallujah, and then receding back to occupy the area in the middle of the city, around the Pizza Slice. It was a vital intersection on Highway 10, a main 4-lane highway leading to the two bridges traversing the Euphrates River to the West and Baghdad to the East.

Battalion 1/8 had been the "tip of the spear" for the entire operation. They busted through the middle of the city, bisecting it and advancing to the southern edge. The southern part of the city opened up to a vast and sparsely vegetated desert, strewn with random mud huts. 1/8 went "firm" near the Water Tower, a prominent terrain feature well seen around the city, skirting the Industrial District. They inevitably sustained the highest casualty rate proceeding the weeks of the battle due to the enemy's incredible commitment to achieve martyrdom. 1/8 carried the immense task of covering huge areas of ground and fighting directly through the heaviest part of the enemy defensive positions – the mouth of the beast, so to speak. The 1/3 Lava Dawgs were adjacent to them, extending to the eastern flank of the city.

1/3 remained North of Highway 10 in the Askari District, which served as a launching point for the attacks on the perimeter of Fallujah along the highways and the Cloverleaf. The Cloverleaf was a cluster of 4 intersecting roundabouts that connected the highways surrounding the city. After being involved in numerous firefights, the battalions had each suffered their share of casualties. Across the two regimental combat teams that made up the conglomeration of all the infantry battalions (RCT-1 and RCT-7) up to that point in the battle, there were estimated to be some 50 Marines killed in action and 400 wounded. This was an impressively low figure when compared to the thousands of dead insurgents littering the Fallujah streets.

The Marines slowly began to appreciate the enormity of the task at hand. Every step on a patrol could be their last. Every charge through a door could be their last. They stacked up with sheer grit, and did not allow reason to affect their resolve. But this was, and will always be, the true essence of Marines – stepping into the unknown for each other, and the country. By now, the enemy had realized their battle was fleeting. They lost their momentum, if they ever had it. The living insurgents likely believed they wasted the six unmolested months to fortify the city, and garner support. As a last resort, insurgent commanders ordered them to seek out martyrdom. Suicide tactics provide the most dangerous and unpredictable tactics to combat. At this time in the city, it became equated to "suicide-by-cop," or much like the Japanese Kamikaze pilots of WWII, who flew their planes into American warships.

Islamic "defensive" jihad can be interpreted as suicide under the guise of an extreme religious commitment. Suicide bombers attempt to kill or maim as many "infidels" as possible. Their strategy was akin to an ancient technique the Spartans' employed at Thermopylae. Use small arms and grenades from a confined defensive covered posture, in order to bottleneck or choke the enemy so as to negate their superior numbers. The same way a badger would defend a hole. No matter how effective this tactic may be in producing horrific results, eventually the martyrs become overwhelmed.

The thought of sacrificing one's life in defense of God's word seemed perplexing to most Americans in Iraq. With a predominantly Christian base, and an illustrious history of risking death to fight wars in the name of freedom, Americans are not inherently eager to die for "God, Country, and Apple Pie." If they must, then they will, but the ultimate goal is to fulfill one's service and duty. Ideally, they and their comrades would rather survive in the process. The warriors of Homer's time were legendary for their glorious feats in battle. As did glory again shed its brightness upon those from the "College of the Crazy Brave."

Fallujah featured and produced some of the finest warriors America has ever had to offer. Those present witnessed extraordinary acts of courage and selfless sacrifice in defense of their brothers. "True glory" was reserved solely for those few who gave it all. But many of the young volunteers didn't fight for glory, they fought for their brothers to live and come home.

Early After Action Reports

The Marines learned lifelong, and lifesaving lessons, quickly. Time was imperative. They had to seize every advantage with overwhelming firepower. Don't risk the lives of Marines when the enemy is located and cornered. Instead, take down the whole fuckin' house. Collateral damage was a political chess game. Young and impressionable warriors feed off of each other during adverse situations. Sap the strength from one to replenish another. Allow the naturally creative leaders to lead, and let the others follow, mimicking the skilled movements of the more seasoned veterans. Carry a dust brush on the flak jacket. There is always time to clean a weapon. Stick an MRE spoon in the gear webbing as well, it's a fashion statement. Do not fire spotting rounds when firing the SMAW, just well-aimed shots. Try to make entry into houses from top-down. Kill zones, like doorways and stairwells, present inevitable dangers. Casualties in a house firefight are nearly unavoidable. By the very nature of the battle, the Marines lacked the simple advantage of flexible repositioning, but compensated through effective cordoning, relentless assaults and firepower.

The lessons continued to mount up together with every mission. The Marines who made it back home still remember even if it's irrelevant now. Remember to remove the thumb clips on the grenades before throwing them. If a door cannot be kicked down by the average grunt, yell for Bean Stalk, and use the biggest guy in the platoon as a battering ram. Throw an incendiary grenade on the engine block of every vehicle. Smash every mirror in the house. Propane tanks and fire will cause harm to anyone in the vicinity. Shoot every dog and cat, especially the mange-covered zombie-like ones. Save the pictures of the dead insurgent's "unhappy bride" for a souvenir. Loot and pillage for as much Iraqi Dinar as can be found. Never assume nobody wants to throw some dice. If anyone finds cash in US currency, be smart and don't tell anyone. Iraqi bills with Saddam's face are obsolete, but cool, nonetheless. Don't assume the occupants of the house are insurgents if they have an AK-47 under their bed, because civilians are permitted to have one per household for protection. Burn every house containing evidence of insurgent activities. Contaminate suspected enemy water and food stores with urine and fecal matter. If there is any suspicion that an insurgent has been in a house, take a dump on the couch. Zero fucks are given and no mercy is offered.

Chapter 6
Mail Call

The Marines could hear the rumble of the AmTracs from several blocks away. The loud Marine carriers meandered to a full stop in front of the CP a few minutes later. The Marines all welcomed Smokey and his crew when they jumped out of the vehicles. Those guys didn't give a fuck. They zipped around the city, hanging out their hatches with reckless abandon. Catching a ride from time to time felt uneasy. The grunts paradoxically viewed the AmTracs as less safe than walking, despite their armor. They were simply bigger targets. But they could go faster than Marines could run, up to 50 mph, and turn on a dime. Ironically, they were amphibious vehicles, operating 300 miles from the nearest ocean, rumbling around a city in the desert. They were multi-functional if nothing else. Overall though, the Marines embraced having them at their disposal.

The AmTracs served as the only armored vehicles available, besides some hastily rigged Humvees, featuring welded steel plating and kevlar blankets. Even yet, the term "armored vehicles" was used very loosely. These were the days before MRAP (Mine Resistant Ambush Protected) vehicles were introduced to the military. This was before the US government spent billions of dollars to properly equip American warfighters serving overseas. The AmTrac commander, Smokey, was a joker, and a bit of a celebrity. He provided endearing motivation for the grunts. Better yet, they always had some goodies with them, like MREs, water, ammo, rockets, grenades, cases of soda, and sometimes Iraqi cigarettes.

Charlie Company felt especially pleased the day they got their first mail call in the city. A mad frenzy erupted as huge boxes and sacks of letters were unloaded from the AmTrac, whilst Marines scrambled for a look at the addresses and names. Country, a stocky, mean-faced, drill instructor type from South Carolina, stood in the middle of the circle that had formed around him. He began yelling out names and throwing their mail across the room. Some guys were lucky enough to get a box thrown at them. Some guys didn't get anything. Those that did receive packages shared with those that didn't. Some of the mail and care packages were sent from churches and elementary schools around the United States. Random letters from school kids would say things like, "Thanks for bein in the Armie" and "my cusin was in the Navie once." Despite the poor spelling, the thought counted greatly.

"We're Marines you dumb fuck, and your cousin is a pussy," responded Animal Mother. "Kids these days don't know shit!" Marines are so raw they'll even chide an 8-year old kid who was just doing a school assignment. Laughs and roars filled the room. There were not any boundaries in the dark humor of grunts. Third Platoon was a bunch of hardcore delinquents. There wasn't much room for sensitivity amongst that crew. After a few minutes, mail call turned into a cacophony of hoots and hollers while the Marines unveiled the contents inside of their parcels. There was beef jerky, Gatorade, mac and cheese, chips, crackers, cookies, candy, razors, toothbrushes, toothpaste, baby wipes, and toilet paper. There was just about all the non-perishable items that anyone could imagine a Marine could use. It felt like Christmas, especially when they realized a few bottles of bourbon had slipped through customs. That evidence was quickly rationed out and consumed. The elated Marines threw around packs of cigarettes, logs of dip, and porn magazines.

They designated a small concrete closet as the "Jerk Room." This provided a location to appreciate some of their more progressive reading materials. They crafted a door from a poncho hanging above the doorway, affixed by some 550 cord. They utilized a cinder block as a chair. Popular porn titles such as "Jugs" and "Milf's over 40" were swapped around. Several of the pages were stuck together. Someone wrote, "Bring your own catch paper" on the wall to remind its patrons of Guy Code. There was absolutely no shame in "rubbing one out" to relieve some stress. It was as common as any other natural function. How could anyone think of jerking off in a combat zone? Dirty hands aren't picky. They hadn't seen women in months. Wooks (female Marines) didn't count. A visual of some T&A goes a long way. The only questions that were asked were, "are you done yet" and "can I borrow that?"

Sitting on the ground, lining the battered walls, were dirty men smelling envelopes. They read in silence. It was impossible to ignore the simplicity of a written letter. The time and care it took to be written. Each word carefully thought out and scripted; folding it, licking the stamp, and send it traveling such a distance to arrive at a plethora of seemingly, undisclosed locations; an APO/FPO (Army Post Office or Fleet Post Office) address. It's a remarkable concept, yet archaic in this digital age. Nothing is faster than an email.

Wildo opened a letter from his girl back home. He missed her, wondered what life was like for her in college at Florida State, and if he and she would be the same. Moke sat beside him, passing him a cigarette. "Man you know I don't smoke," Wildo replied. "Yeah but, it looks cool, don't it", Moke sneered. Nah, I just like the smell of them, when they're not burning. That's weird, right", as Wildo put the cigarette to his lips to taste the menthol on the filter. She sent some pictures of her and her friends at the FSU football game. They were dressed in short shorts, spirited colors, and face paint. The men reveled at the sheer ignorance of college kids, with their keggers and frat parties. It was a world away from this broken town. "Ohhhh …

what's up with her friend, she has a big nose, but I'd smash it," Moke joked. "She's a coke whore! She'd let you too," snickered Wildo.

Infantry life was raw. Emotion was covertly minimal. There was a numbing effect to combat. The mind and body intrinsically shut down to preserve the most necessary emotions, fear and excitement (adrenaline). Exhibiting the fight or flight mechanisms that have led human beings to evolve to their zenith. Morbid humor and anger were just the temporary fallout, residual by-products of that fear, that fiending addiction. A thousand new drug addicts were created overnight. Each individual had to muster themselves, to keep their bearings, to temper the bloody, flash floods that gushed through their veins and kept their hearts from exploding out from their chests.

In the subsequent weeks, the Marines relocated a few more times. They spent a few days operating in an affluent neighborhood, where the streets featured two and three-story mansions, equivalent to the Hollywood Hills of Fallujah. Huge walled compounds with open courtyards and swaths of well irrigated grass and manicured vegetation. Inside some homes, were large marble staircases that ascended to a balcony and an atrium with vaulted ceiling and tile. Each platoon spread throughout the house. It was the first time, in the weeks since D-Day that they were able to truck in hot A-rations. It was basically a glorified MRE from a can, but cooked in the chow hall and served hot. There were no complaints. Their taste buds were deprived flavor for so long, anything hot and salty tasted gourmet. They operated there for a few days, patrolling, and returning to their luxurious accommodations at day's end. They almost felt guilty for their comforts. The less they had, the less they took for granted. The grunts' mantra, "It can always be worse," firmly applied.

As Thanksgiving was just days away and the men looked forward to the glorious spread on which they would feast. After a few days of hot, rations for dinner, they were getting used to their accommodations. It was apparent the Marines would spend the holidays in Fallujah, and thus the remainder. No one was going home for Christmas. They were unaware that their vision of holiday tide would be forever tainted from spending a winter there. It was getting colder by the night, colder than even the most astute, logistical officer had planned for; down to 20 degrees Fahrenheit in the darkness. Who would've thought it gets that cold in the desert? The hours of fire watch during the night produced mind numbing, hallucinations.

As one Marine sat shivering at his post at 0300, he exclaimed, "Why are deserts so cold at night and so hot during the day?"

Often, the temperature dropped fifty to sixty degrees within 24 hours. The extreme changes in temperature prevented most things from growing, creating a desert – a metaphor for the antiquated culture of Babylon. Geography, history and culture baffled the Marine. He thought of unsolved equations scribbled on chalkboards, connecting information to reason. He wanted to attend college after his tour. He wanted the answers to his questions. He wanted to replace the persuasion of an M16 with the indisputable power of an arsenal of knowledge.

Just days later, after getting used to their luxurious amenities, the Company abandoned their affluent abode for a more permanent firm base. Apparently, a nearby schoolhouse would provide the ideal fixed position from which to operate, rather than their current five-star accommodation. They removed rows and rows of chairs and desks, and neatly reorganized them, covered and aligned in the courtyard. Sandbagging the windows was always a priority, along with building bunkered emplacements for guard posts, tactically positioned around the perimeter. A short concrete wall surrounding the schoolyard provided little protection from insurgent attacks. A well-placed RPG shot from the surrounding blocks would blast right through the double walled sand bags. This provided their best chance, though, until heavy machinery came in to build HESCO barriers. Nobody believed that would happen in the short term. The interior walls revealed graffiti and other drawings created in pencil and crayon. In one of the rooms, they even found a drawing depicting a plane crashing into a building. "You see? They are breeding little terrorists," one Marine exclaimed. Kids are so impressionable they thought. The Marines felt shocked. Yet, they were not oblivious to their own government's propaganda.

The ice-cold nights rendered most of the Marines insomniacs. They needed to raid the surrounding houses during patrols for blankets to stave off the frigid air seeping into their bones. They began improvising sources of heat by building fire pits in rusted oil drums with makeshift chimneys to filter the toxic air that would otherwise hover stagnantly in the room. They ignored the smoke to compensate for warmth, which had incurred them during the nights. The "firewatch" was bestowed the added responsibility of replenishing the fire with wood and watching that it didn't extinguish. As they awoke each morning, they found their faces covered with black soot. Photographs depict young men, old and dirty. They had aged many years in just a few weeks.

The grunts are a culture of seniority. Marines have a propensity to seek leaders that are outspoken, with an unflinching exterior. From day one on those yellow footprints, it is drilled into their brains to take initiative, to volunteer for everything, and exploit every opportunity to take charge. Leadership billets, along with rank, had its privileges. Every day, even in a combat zone, there is the infamous trickle-down phenomenon of "working parties". The order comes from the top, and younger boots are exploited. It's not a festive social gathering at all, but rather, more akin to forced labor. It ranges from all types of miscellaneous deeds that must be done for the benefit of the entire unit. As an example, loading or unloading vehicles, digging holes and filling sandbags, burning excrement, etc. It is subscribed that leaders must be assertive enough to order others into this repeated submission.

"Boots" are generally termed as an unlimited source of labor for activities considered beneath that of a "saltier" enlisted type. The logic being, everyone has been there, and must earn their way out of perpetual "bootness". "Gimme three bodies", was their party invitation; subjugating them as expendable and disposable entities. Invariably, in the absurdity of it all, higher command insists that these boots be given the proper title of Marine, as if it alleviates them from the reality that they are insignificant. There is never enough boots to cycle through all that is required by the company agenda, so inevitably, they may be chosen two or three times in a day to perform some type of unwanted obligation. It was ridiculous and monotonous. It was frowned upon that anyone carrying a leadership billet would volunteer themselves, ahead of a boot to perform such menial tasks. Leaders were expected to have the balls to be relentless in this pursuit. Their mantra was a paradox.

Privates eat first. Never exploit those who trust enough to follow. Never wager money with juniors or get put in a position to take from them. Maintain bearing when you lead. Maintain discipline when you follow. Action leads to reaction, inaction leads to consequence. Never underestimate the gravity placed on attitude. Morale is the greatest weapon and the most contagious disease. Great leaders lead by example all the time, unyielding to complacent behavior. Negative leaders give into their vices and make justifications. Those boots, juniors, or underestimated types seen to be inferior, are usually the ones who exhibit the most bravery, daring, and inspiration to their fellow Marines. Combat has a weird way of producing the best or the worst in human character. It reflects the truest test of merit.

The Marines settled into the new routine of a different firm base. Patrols went out and came back in, several blocks of houses cleared and re-cleared; photographically memorizing every detail of the surrounding environment; slash marks and scribbles on a map, working parties, the consistent application of more fortifications, cleaning, and maintenance. The general rule was "weapon, gear, self"...in that order. It was the first and last things a Marine did each day. Dust off weapons and lube them up. The bolt sliding with smooth action...a clean weapon was a reliable one. Accommodate gear, replenish grenades, smoke, and flares, adjust pouches and incidentals as per the mission, refill and top off water, stage all gear, covered and aligned, neat and tidy. They were like firemen, who pre-position their boots, gear, and fire retardant wardrobe next to the fire engine. When the call comes in, they step right into action with a single fluid motion, never wasting a step. This was the duty of the react platoon, who was in a constant state of alertness to respond and reinforce other patrols in the area.

During their down time, thoughts of the yule tide were drawing near. Mothers and daughters back home peeked out the window as husbands and fathers shoveled snow, absent from their sons in a desert town. There wasn't opportunity for the Marines to stop by a Macy's or any other randomly commercialized, department store. They were exempt from the daunting task of holiday shopping lists and gift wrapping, but their APO/FPO address made outgoing postage available to the Marines, free of charge.

Groucho creatively fixed the idea of cutting postcards from MRE boxes. An ingenious substitution for a Hallmark card, he mastered the equal sized, rectangular shaped pieces of cardboard, and sketched an impressionable backdrop of the Fallujah city skyline. The illustration highlighted the irony of a "Christmas in Fallujah", depicting solid, geometrically simple, concrete structures and mosques riddled with bullet holes, burned out vehicles, and a torrent of rockets and fire from the sky. After several had been made, their popularity amongst the Marines had increased the demand for more. Groucho worked feverishly on his spare time to accommodate the requests. After sketching them, he encouraged the Marines to individually personalize his work with crayons found in the school's supply closet. It was a hit.

Reporters got wind of the phenomenon and stopped by the firm base to interview him. It was a wonderfully, positive story to share with the families back home. Groucho, humble and gracious, was a little apprehensive to revel in his creative talents. It was a huge morale booster. A poignant moment for the Marines sending them and for the families back home, receiving them. They were galvanized by the comforting message that was so reflective of their son's faithful service. It showed the indomitable spirit of selfless sacrifice. The cost of equipping and training a Marine for war....$50,000. The cost of postage for an MRE postcard with an APO address....Free. The look on a Mom's face in Smallville, USA when she reads the words of her son from a war zone...Priceless.

Chapter 7
The Water Tower (Queens)

As soon as the Marines finished fortifying the schoolhouse, Command ordered Charlie Company to pack up and move south across MSR Fran (Highway 10) to relieve Battalion 1/8. After nearly four weeks of continuous fighting through the staunchly defended heart of the city, 1/8 sustained over fifty percent casualties and was rendered combat ineffective. The Lava Dawgs of 1/3 were ordered to relieve them at their embattled firm base position, near the Water Tower. US missiles and artillery had severely damaged the Water Tower during the bombardment. The underground lines were punctured, spewing water, and flooding every street in the surrounding blocks. Firm Base Pickering, as it would later be named in the Marine's honor, was a former schoolhouse, and very heavily defended by bunkers and Hesco barriers. Previously, 1/8 utilized the property as a temporary motor pool for AAVs and Humvees, which provided them extra comfort, knowing they had some "heavy" assets nearby.

Making the trek to the South presented a panoramic view of the scope and level of destruction the city sustained in the fighting. Encumbering potholes, cement barriers, and huge pieces of broken concrete littered the 4 lanes of Highway 10, which bisected the city. Air strikes had completely demolished the four and five-story buildings. Minarets that once shadowed a mosque were downed, and miles of wire from fallen power lines stretched across the streets. It seemed as if every wall and building and vehicle had been riddled with bullet holes or worse. One by one, the AmTracs shuttled the Marines back and forth to their new position, maneuvering around the sand berms and concertina wire that guarded the entranceway to FB Pickering. Battalion 3/5 was assuming control of the entire area North of Fran, which included 1/3's former AO in the Askari District. Battalion 3/1 shared some responsibilities to the North as well, but was to redeploy back to the outskirts of the city. Meanwhile, 1/8 prepared to head back home to North Carolina, having been in country for seven months and suffered many casualties.

The Marines from Charlie 1/3 exited the AmTracs, looking around at their new home. A few members of 1/8 remained intently focused on a game of spades. The droves from Charlie funneled in, quickly traversing narrow spaces between the barriers, inspecting their vacancies before they were vacated. The 1/8 Marines barely gave them a glance, aged, sour faced, and careless to the commotion happening around them. They didn't speak a word, donned with headphones from an Ipod, flipping and shuffling cards, just killing time until the hours passed to leave the city. They were all Infantry Marines, with shared grievances, mentality and swagger, but the unwritten rule was "Fuck you, if you're not one of us!". The premise of unit integrity firmly applied. So no conversation was given and no questions were to be asked or answered. They didn't give a fuck.

The Charlie 1/3 guys had their own egos to worry about. Everyone knew what they (1/8) had been through and a silent respect was conveyed. It was weird, almost intimidating. They lost a lot of guys. There is nothing to say. They didn't want to know them, they didn't want to show them around, or even shake hands. They were coined "brothers" under a title, but after battle, they didn't trust anyone, not even their own kind. The bond is just between the small clique of guys that shared intimate space for all those dirty days. It didn't matter anyway. Soon Charlie Corps would take this battle space and be responsible for it. Now they were in the thick of it. The word was they (1/8) had a lot of problems with snipers in the area, and one in particular who was rumored to be a Chechnyan with blonde hair and blue eyes. "Isn't that near Russia? Wait?....but they're Muslim fighters"? Many of them had no idea where Chechnya was or their most recent involvement in the Balkans War in the 90's and Kosovo. A true Jihad would command all Islamists as their duty to answer the call to defend any Muslim land. This, indeed, included traveling from hundreds and thousands of miles away from their homelands to fight for Islam, traversing different borders, ethnic, and cultural lines. They were united entirely under the presumption of religion.

The area surrounding FB Pickering looked like a wasteland of flattened houses on all sides. The entrance to the firm base featured a narrow winding road of berms and barriers leading to the ECP (entry control point) to slow oncoming traffic, not that there would be any civilian vehicles driving about. Large holes dotted the sides of the schoolhouse walls, created by RPG rounds, an eerie reminder that a lucky RPG could ruin anybody's day. The firm base bordered the obliterated intersections of a once sprawling neighborhood frequented by frolicking children and businessmen alike. Upon the arrival of the 1/3 Marines, the area around the Water Tower was enveloped in a day and night fight to repel the insurgent onslaught of RPGs as the Marines defended their embattled positions at the firm base. Charlie Company would remain embedded there for at two more months.

As the sun began to set on their first night in FB Pickering, two RPGs slammed into the compound – "BOOM, BOOM!" Marines scattered to find cover and return fire. Six-foot berms of sand and debris surrounded the perimeter, topped with concertina wire. Any insurgent foolish enough to try to breach the wire would be slowed down enough for the Charlie machine-gunners to easily dispatch him. The rooftops featured two bunkers positioned diagonally across from one another, armed with M240G machine-guns. Three more guard posts were scattered around the perimeter and main entrance. The impressive sound of the 240s rang out and a few heavy assault men returned fire with the SMAW. None of the Marines pinpointed the source of the rockets, and the perpetrators vanished as fast as they appeared. The newly arrived Marines immediately deployed a patrol in order to track them down, only to find no one.

Life at the firm base differed greatly from the previous weeks of virtually continuous offensive action. Hours of boredom was mixed in with 15 minutes of excitement and terror. It just didn't feel right to even leave a covered overhead position. To hygiene and shit, they were the most vulnerable. They had to go out in flack and kevlar in case something went down. They had nylon covered tents, with field expedient toilets out in the middle of the courtyard of the base. There was absolutely no protection and always a wonder no one ever fell victim to a lucky sniper shot while taking a shit. Some guys took their chances with comfort and neatly removed and staged their gear outside of the tent. "If I'm gonna get shot taking a shit, I'm gonna die comfortable. The nerve racking anxiety...getting scoped in the crosshairs of some random hadji hate-filled, jihadi, blue eyed, sniper, right now! I'm all itchy and shit". Don't look around too much, and take a round in the head. Just stay deliberate and do what needs to be done.

Patrols departed by day and by night, as each platoon took turns and cycled through the rotation. The squads would run the gauntlet of fire, slogging through the stagnant and putrefied water with floating dog carcasses and rotting sewage. The streets were saturated with infested filth, death, and decay.

The Water Tower loomed overhead. Depending on the position of the sun, it would be a reflector beam or a daunting silhouette. One could see it from anywhere in the city. It stood in the area known as Queens, and provided to the ground commanders of both sides a well-known terrain feature, a landmark. The tower bordered a massive junk yard and car repair shops, truck equipment suppliers, and welder shops. For this, it became known as the Industrial District. Fallujah served as the go-to place to fix a flat tire, repair an engine, or change the oil. Bordering the main highways running through Central Iraq, the area was a prime hub for all things legitimately or illegitimately related.

During the nights, operations were limited. It wasn't a common practice to clear houses at night, unless absolutely necessary. It was risky. The night operation equipment that the Marines had was limited as well. Tac lights and night vision goggles, usually outdated hand-me-downs from the Army, untenable, and cumbersome. NVGs were better served for observation from static posts, but moving through houses at night presented a whole array of different challenges. The minute they switch on flashlights, they lose the tactical initiative if they are not extremely fast and deliberate. They didn't have enough adequate training in urban night ops. At least that is how it was in 2004 depending on the unit. However, the squads were still tasked to run patrols night and day. They would stretch out for several blocks, changing up the route, zigzagging, and uncovering new things that were previously overlooked. Some sheds and garage doors still had locks on them. It could be an insurgent weapons cache, that tin can, plastic bag, or piece of garbage could be an IED.

Weed ingeniously attached zip ties to M79 fragmentation grenades in order to blow locks off of doors and gateways. The tactic proved extremely effective in the event that the bird shot from the Mossberg shotguns were ineffective. They received getting hot chow every night for dinner. The Marines of 1/3 began to see the light at the end of the tunnel. Only days into their new home, life became more predictable, comfortable, and sustainable. Hot cocoa at night even became a regular occurrence. Country would roll up another ball of C4 and light it with a Bic. "Hey, ya'll get back now, I'm making cocoa," he would say. Boxes of non-perishable packages steadily arrived in the mail, just in time for the frigid nights.

Probes outside the wire bring little results. All seems quiet at night. Everybody just wants to step it out back to a cement floor and warm blanket. The Mujahadeen moved at night. They owned it because they know where the Marines were not going to be. Fire watch kept an eye out. Security is the foundation they are built on. Any one Marine could be entrusted with the safety of the whole company at night. To stand guard, stay vigilant while the others rest and recuperate for the clearing days ahead. Everyone took their turns, from squad leader down, Corporal to PFC, day and night, to faithfully execute the duties of post.

By now, the grunts knew what to expect. Now it was just a matter of time, counting the days, weeks, and months. It was tallying a small pocket-book calendar and grid squares. Waiting for some guy with a pistol holster and a cigar to walk the line and say yea or nay. He pulled up in his fleet of armored up Humvees, humming the Hymn. The Marines pepped up, not with absolute reverence, just toeing the line. He presented the bright idea to use their thin skinned, high back Humvees for night time mounted patrols, driving in "black out." Driving at night in black out meaning (no headlights) was unfamiliar to all but the most seasoned military drivers. They could not ignore the very real risk of getting lost, especially if the shit hit the fan while they were out. It was a cluster fuck waiting to happen.

The Mujahadeen would often trail behind the Marines on a patrol, unbeknownst to them. They crept close to the firm base through the maze of back alleys, in defilade from view of the 240 machine gun positions. The patrols had to keep a constant pressure to deny the insurgents freedom of movement and ability to operate close to the base, in the unlikely event they were able to get off a well-placed rocket shot into FB Pickering.

While inside the Hesco walled, compound, the threats from the outside somewhat, subsided. If someone had procured a little down time, they had a few simple pleasures. There was candy, cigarettes, and piano cleaner. It was sold and used to remove dirt from weapons, but also huffed for a 20 second head rush. Ipods were still a relatively new phenomenon, digitally advanced to its predecessor, The Walkman. Some guys stayed glued to anything they could, temporary ear muffs distracted them with a beat. Music took them somewhere else, more than a book. Intangible and nostalgic rhythms take them back to a time maybe not so different.

"Hey, so does Fallujah remind you of being home, back on the block"? Being from Union City, NJ, Casper replied "Shit nigga...dey ain't shooting rockets in da hood"!!! Hailing from the mean streets of Harlem, Merc saved the main meals from his MREs. He covered his face with a desert camo, neck pull up. All that could be seen was his big eyes popping out from a pair of steel framed classes. X had the street in his veins, expertly detailed with a sense for sniffing stuff out. He had amassed an extensive collection of watches confiscated from "suspected" enemy houses. He was always talking about "snow bunnies" and MMA fights. X had the Haitian connection with 8 Ball. From the inner city streets of tough American cities like Baltimore and New York, they spoke a French Creole dialect. 8 Ball was strong as a bull, but rarely said a word. X tried to prove he could breathe through his eyelids while he talked.

Night comes around and they load up for a blackout Humvee, expedition. At 0200, they saddle up and disembark into the dark abyss of Fallujah's alleyways. A trippy- green, tunnel vision, circle of light, turned night into day. Dogs ran the streets, the glowing of several pairs of eyeballs, like fire flies. They followed the stench, wafting in the chilled air, of rotting corpses half submerged in mud puddles. Turn left, then right, then left...through mud holes and over fallen concrete walls. They don't really know where they are going, just looking for known terrain features, merely black and white structures with photogenic flashes of burned out vehicles and recollected features on backdrops and street corners. They kept driving in circles of grid squares. Radio contact, radio check, and then turn the volume down.

There was the continuous humming of the Humvees, as American craftsmanship gurgled and slurped JP8. The nights were so silent that none of their movements were secret or stealthy. Hubris had faded a bit. "We can't see shit, can't hear shit, and there is not much to report" Wait it out and flush them out in the morning. Cordon off the block, and carry on with the plan of the day.

That next morning on patrol, Second Platoon stumbled upon a huge cache of old anti-aircraft guns, mortars, and WWII era, rusted German MG-42s and other assorted small arms. It appears the insurgents tried to employ anything they could, even 60 year old, inoperable relics. They looked cool though. It was the kind of thing that brought out the imagination of a young boy growing up with dreams of glory on some distant battlefield. The artillery pieces and shells were piled and scattered about under a solitary roofed building in the middle of a large muddy, field underneath the Water Tower. The Marine operations were easily observed. Tanks and other supporting armor liked setting up near large open spaces, giving them longer fields of fire and a chance to put their imaging sights to better use. There were so many little crevices for a retinal to scan, tangled in a myriad of angles and spaces, shadowed and obscured.

The grunts took pride in their skills at range estimation. Thumps from 203s mark designated spots for directing fires. A typical day of contact with the enemy would start out by cordoning off a city block, walking the streets, and systematically, entering and clearing every house, every room, and every space. Pot shots would ring out from out yonder in the distance, then again, getting closer. If the shots are coming near their direction, it would surely be heard in a different context. Bullets have distinctively different sounds when fired at them, as opposed to being fired from them. The only thing the Marines hear when firing the round, is the recoil sound of springs and gas being pulled through the guts of the weapon. However, down range, the whipping snap of an AK round echoing off walls is an encapsulating, adrenaline-filled orgasm of fear and excitement. If it's going the other way, it's more of a muffled pop. In that respect, there is little doubt when receiving "incoming" fire. First thing that is said, "Where the fuck is that coming from...anybody see a flash", the usual collectively, expressed lingo.

In the event the sniper is detected, M203 gunners use 40mm grenades to mark the suspected location and then everyone orients their wrath on that point. It's a beautiful thing. Needless to say, the M203 gunners serve a light, short ranged artillery function. They could pop those babies out 400 meters and sometimes more if they lobbed them high enough. Take out whole rooms from the outside of a house with a well-placed shot through a window. The unbelievable tempo of combat pushes a man to become extremely proficient in the wake of a small amount of trial and error. In training, they always go slow and methodical, checking safety systems, using instruments, and allotting a very limited supply of ammunition. Now, these salty ass grunts are trying to give away ammo to their buddies and give them the guilt trip about "spread loading" to equal the weight. With a seemingly unlimited supply of ammunition, they expended as much as they had, whenever possible.

Chapter 8
Twelve Days of Christmas

They woke up where they had crashed the night before. It was yet another unfamiliar residence, but it was their inhospitable accommodations for the night. Slumped against the walls, covered in poncho liners, the sun had not yet arose to lubricate the transition from sub-consciousness to vigilance. Sleepy eyes crack open, and a seemly benign voice just screams in silence. This particular morning was unsettling. The main effort of Charlie Company 1/3 had pushed out from FB Pickering the day before on an overnight patrol to disrupt enemy activity and search and re-clear the remainder of the blocks along Henry, the North/South phase line between Battalions 1/3 and 3/1. The always trusted, Weapons Platoon had left elements behind to safeguard the FB, mostly the machine gunners.

Their supporting elements, especially the (0351s) Assault Men, were invaluable for their demolition and rocket capabilities. Hence, they were evenly divided teams that would break off from their respective platoon, and attach themselves to other platoons. In the military world of MOS (Military Occupational Specialty), different jobs require different functions, and the (0311s) Riflemen, worked in close contact with their fellow infantry support units, including (0331s) Machine Guns and (0341s) Mortars. Together they packed a lethal punch.

Starting from Highway 10 (PL Fran), they continued the "squeegee effect", pushing south, on a re-re-clearing mission. Preacher would always brief the platoon in a geeky, little voice like, "the Command was so happy with our performance the other day, that they want us to go back and do it again". Groans and growls followed abruptly with hisses and snarls. It was still new operating territory. Every building had some type of destruction to it. None were left unscathed, grim reminders of the fierce fighting for Battalion 1/8. They were traversing the same ground, ready to tangle with the last of the hardcore resistance.

After 5 weeks into the battle, any Mujahadeen still running around, hiding and scheming, were either trapped or making ready for some type of martyrdom, with a suicidal ambush from a barricade. They were suffering. There was no question about that. The insurgents had been cut-off, surrounded, out of food, water, supplies, and caches were dwindled. The enemy fighters still holding out were the most committed and dangerous, because they were fully intent on dying and taking Marines with them.

It was designated Block 851 on the intel map that had been allocated to them. The neighborhood consisted of two story houses lining the main two lane road (PL

Henry) which bisected to the North with Highway 10 (PL Fran). The end of the blocks heading to the East opened up to a large empty field, surrounded by other homes and higher level apartment and some commercial buildings. It was a prominent area for merchant activity and contained strategically important routes for the insurgency. The Euphrates River was less than a mile away to the West. The area known as the Pizza Slice was just 200 meters north of their position in 851. It split them apart from the main artery into two separate veins leading to the only two bridges that traversed the river, in or out of Fallujah. Naturally, it was among the heaviest concentration of fighting early on in the battle because of its location within the South of the city and its close proximity to the river. Accordingly, it still remained a significant threat to the safety of the Marine's SASO (Stability and Support Operations), which had technically been underway since mid-November.

The, infamous, Government Building loomed to the North, next to a large mosque directly on PL Fran. It was a skyline feature that was used as a northerly azimuth in terms of terrain association and orientation. The platoons mustered together with weapons slung and a hand in their pocket, alternating them to keep warm. The sun slowly rose above the crest of the rooftops. Shivering from the frigidly, dry air, they passed around a pack of Iraqi cigarettes, the Miami brand. That was weird they were called Miami. It was definitely random, but that was how everything in Iraq seemed to be...random. They tasted like a wimpy, Marlboro Red without the abrasive scratch down the throat that "Cowboy Killers" often give. The flipping and clanking of the Zippo lit them up, inducing a few heavy drags, inhaling from the butt of the cigarette, while simultaneously, exhaling from the nose. Those were the true smokers. Every anxiety-filled drag put a calming flow to their involuntary, muscle twitches. The dippers and chewers (smokeless tobacco) huddled around, sticking their grubby-filled fingers into a fresh, cardboard can of Copenhagen from the States. Pinching out a fatty and slipping it neatly between their gums. That first juicy, brown spit was the best part.

They get their order to step off, splitting up the company into platoons, then platoons break off into squads, fanning out down individual neighborhood streets. The squads communicated with some low grade, hand-me-down, head strap communication gear that rubbed blisters into the side of the face and ear of anyone wearing it. It rarely performed its function. Supplemented by some hand-held, walkie-talkies; it wasn't really "high speed" gear. Staying current on the happenings on "the net" was a job in of itself. Making sure to stay on-line in the sweeps, as to not get too far ahead or behind of each other to avoid possible fratricide if they ran into something. It was tedious, monotonous, and abruptly vicious. It was all the descriptive synonyms that end in -ous.

First Platoon split up. Only made up of less than two squads, they each took a separate neighborhood street, bounding from house to house, and zigzagging over the rocky asphalt to hit the opposite houses on the other side. PL Henry bordered the AO of other rifle companies from other battalions, so it was a busy day of multiple operations and patrols taking place at the same time. There was a sizable presence by the Marines with CAAT vehicles, AmTracs, and tanks, all working in coordination. Firepower was just a shout away for a grunt in need of some heavier assets. The block the Marines from First Platoon Charlie were clearing contained about 10-12 houses on each side until they ended into a large, open field, effectively a "dead end". Anything or anyone caught flushed out into that field was an easy kill, so it was a strategic pinch.

      The two squads would push down, clearing, and if the enemy appeared they would ultimately get trapped. Third platoon was on a group of rooftops to the West, their guns covering another avenue escape route. The cordon of the area was methodical. The alleyways and byways supported their elusive escapes, and mouse holes connecting extensive trail systems behind walls. Moving from West to East, First Squad was to the North and Second Squad to the South. Fish's squad had been half assembled back together since the ambush earlier on November 13. Six were so severely wounded, that they never returned. Four others had recovered from their shrapnel wounds and were eager to get back to help out their short-handed Marines. Following treatment of their wounds, Cherokee and Lanky returned the next day, and Bull was back within a week. However, Blanton had been out for a month recovering at BAS (Battalion Aid Station), Bravo Surgical, refusing to be flown back to the US for surgery, after being shot in the foot and almost severing his pinky toe.

      With those who returned, First Squad were a fire team plus. Blanton was an Assault man (0351) attached to Fish's squad, and he had just returned that same day from a month in BAS. He had eagerly requested to be returned to the line weeks earlier and was frustrated he had been away from the rest of the guys for that long. It was a completely natural feeling, especially when Marines have the kind of character that Blanton did. A 20 year old Georgia native, he stepped off the AmTrac earlier that morning before the mission kicked off, with a huge grin on his face, and all the guys riled around him, with roars and slaps on the back.

      When they started the patrols that day, he insisted on being the point man for the day's clearing. He felt he owed a debt to what was left of First Squad, because they were still around gutting it out every day and short on trigger pullers. As they cleared the first 5 or 6 houses on the short block, it neared to the end of the road where the houses stopped, forming into a huge open field. The houses from the other block, their back patios were inches away. There wasn't much space in between houses and apparently the neighbors didn't give themselves much privacy.

No one really understood why there was such randomness to the development of the neighborhoods in Fallujah. Some of the affluent seemed immaculately structured, while others had no rhyme or reason...just nothingness, a no man's land, with sparsely unfinished brick frames scattered about. The spacious dirt field became the end of any escape route, because any insurgent trying to run the 400 meter swath of open area was just going to die tired.

Pink Panther was the hawk on the rooftops. He owned the city skyline. Lava Dawg snipers from Weapons Company 1/3 covered the entire battalion's ass on clearing patrols. When the grunts kicked in the doors, and flushed the hadgis out, Pink and Styx would lay them down.

Fish began pushing his squad over to the second to last house. Blanton led the way, kicking in the door which immediately opened to a set of stairs going straight up to the second level, sort of like a cement loft apartment. At the top of the stairs was a doorway on the right and a short hallway to the left. Blanton charged up the stairs leading the squad; turning to his right into the first room, the door was cracked open. He stepped in and a burst of machine gun fire from the corner of the room hit him in the upper torso and neck. He died instantly.

Five insurgents were hunkered in the room in a hasty position. The rest of First Squad was still pushing up the stairs when the shocking barrage of gunfire threw them all back, rolling down onto one another like dominos. In the confusion they pulled out just outside the door to the stairway. "He's still up there" they screamed! They didn't know Blanton was already dead. The other assault men who were outside immediately punched a rocket into the window of the room. Malik, Cherokee, and Fish, quickly reassembled after Fernando's blast and charged back up the stairs. At the top, Blanton lay lifeless and his M-16 was gone.

Malik quickly oriented into the room with the semi-stagnant smoke billowing from it, but there was no one there. The enemy had run out the back to the patio and hopped the walls, scattering in different directions. Weed was sighted in through the aperture of his rifle from a rooftop behind the narrow alleyway , across the block. It was just enough clearing for him to witness the situation. Weed saw them running and jumping roofs, triggering a few rounds off from his M16 rifle while the insurgents were on the hop-skippity. He got the last one running in the chest, dropping him in the courtyard, before getting to the wall. When Fish's squad realized the situation and got to the patio, there was an older bald man in his mid to late fifties, just bleeding out with an AK next to him. They searched him and he had a roll of American dollars in his pockets. The other insurgents had split up, and Fish's squad regrouped for a plan to pursue them. Second Squad, First Platoon was on the rooftop, across the street, where Weed had taken the shot on the old man. It was the limit of advance, and a perfect vantage point to support the escalating situation.

It came over the radio on Bean Stalk's PRC-19, a term they had only heard a few times before, KIA. They didn't say his name, just his kill number. Everyone had a "kill number" sharpied onto their shoulder pockets. It was a number that would identify them when they were dead or seriously wounded. It was always a shock to hear about a guy who was gone, when they might have had just hours earlier, shared a pre-mission cigarette or ate an MRE together.

First Squad carried Blanton out on a bed sheet they found in one of the rooms. A contingent from Moke's squad ran over to pay respects, render support, and coordinate a plan. Still in shock and grief stricken for a fallen comrade, it was one of those unexplainable moments full of every kind of emotion. It had been a month almost exactly to the day that First Squad got hit on Nov. 13. First Platoon took a moment and gathered their bearings. They loaded Blanton's body onto an AmTrac, the door lifted, and it clanked away slowly turning the corner.

They saddled up to continue the fight and formulated a plan. There was nowhere for the enemy to run, they were trapped. They already had the insurgents cornered in the last house. Payback was an inevitable condition. Malik wasn't about to let these guys get away. They taunted the trapped enemy, cursing them, and lobbing random grenades from all sides of the house. The enemy knew they would die, but the Marines had the option to minimize their own casualties. They had control of the initiative. By this time, the rest of Charlie Company was on scene, scouring the skyline from other nearby sectors and rooftops. Charlie had the place on lock down.

Wildo's fire team ran back from First Squad's position in the aftermath of Blanton's departure. There was a convoy of up armored Humvees all lined up, watching and waiting. They were Marines from 3/1. It looked like they weren't doing much and a Marine was just standing aimlessly behind a .50 caliber machine gun. One of the Marines from the team running by was like "Hey man, you want to get some trigger time on that thing, we need some help down here". He turned around and a bright shining flash of a gold leaf glistened off of his collar. His reply was "fuck yeah". There was no mention of rank or any of that fake respect bullshit. It was kind of odd and surprising to see a field grade officer in the turret of a Humvee.

The grunts kept pushing to the next block leading the way, as the Major ordered his driver to follow them down the street to the target house. They pointed over in the direction, "yeah just light that house up all over". He oriented the heavy mounted machine gun, pressing his thumbs on the butterfly trigger, firing from side to side, chipping huge chunks of wall, and blowing out the window sills with the hypnotic sound of a heavily powered, belt fed weapon. After exhausting two full ammo cans, he yelled, "I'm out" and waved as the Humvee reversed back down the street, with hoots and hollers of gratitude in return from the 11's.

Second Squad was across the street from the target house in an over watch position, ready in support. The remaining remnants of First Squad gallantly regrouped to carry the burden of a top down assault on the target house. They hopped the walls from the house where they were originally ambushed earlier in the day. Crouched together in a perfect, low silhouetted stack, they moved slow and steady towards a door framed covering of a stairwell that led from the roof, down into the house where the insurgents were expecting their martyrdom. Malik, Fish, Cherokee, and Lanky approached cautiously, as an insurgent poked out and ripped a burst of gunfire over their heads, missing them by inches. Lanky fell back, lost his balance, and fell off the roof. Bean Stalk was there quickly to pick him up.

Simultaneously, after the enemy fired on Fish's squad, the rest of First Platoon opened up with all they had, spraying from an L-shape position, as Fernando fired a rocket from the shoulder, completely obliterating the covered entrance way to the stairs. The stairs collapsed and debris filled in the gaps. They would have to attempt to re-enter from the bottom level. By now the target house was just one story, all shot up, and filled with holes. It was hard to believe the enemy was alive and still fighting in their collapsing tomb. A few more rockets in the bottom level opened some holes to see inside. It was dark and cloudy with smoke and dust. It appeared the insurgents were in the back part of the kitchen. First squad re-grouped for a third time, stacked along the side of the house. Bean Stalk, a giant of a radioman joined up with the stack as well.

Suddenly, Wildo started triggering a full magazine into the bottom level of the other house, directly adjacent to the target house. "I got that fucker, man. Did you see him running, crouching by those windows? I'm going down there". Wildo rushed down the stairs from the roof of Second Squad's position. Assertively in his step, he rumbled across the street with Moke and two SAW gunners, 8 Ball and Merc, following in trace. They approached the long driveway, the gate had already been blasted out and the house was already cleared before. When the insurgent cell split up from ambushing Fish's squad, one of them got separated alone in the other house.

Wildo and Moke approached at the ready as 8 Ball and Merc covered the windows and the sides. It was a weird scene. One of the insurgents was lying flat on his back in the main doorway to the two story house. He was wearing a white pair of Addidas and khaki pants. They couldn't see the rest of him, only from mid-thigh down to his feet. He wasn't moving, so they started to shoot at his feet to see if he was dead. Wildo shot off one of the guy's shoes and slowly the bleeding foot began to recede back into the house from the doorway. They were a bit perplexed to the awkward scene. He was still moving, but really slow. They stood clear of the kill zone in the doorway because it was very possible the wounded enemy was lying down with his weapon transfixed on the doorway as soon as the Marines attempted to make entry. That first man could have needlessly been shot. Instead, Moke pulled the pin on a grenade, and bounced it off the doorway, landing almost on top of the body. They pulled around the wall..."Boom".

As the smoke cleared, the body was gone. They freaked out thinking the guy had gotten up and ran away before the grenade exploded. Poking around the corner, the insurgent was blown 10 feet back into the house with a huge gash in his side spilling out a pool of blood. They went in clearing the bottom level, a kitchen and dining area. Directly behind that house was the house where they killed Blanton. It was eerie. The insurgent had attempted to partially barricade the doorway with an old bicycle. Wildo tossed it into the driveway like a trash bag. As Moke covered the extraction from the house with the rest of the team, Wildo man handled the insurgent by one of his feet. With his right hand on his weapon, he bear clawed the dead enemy with his other hand and dragged the150lbs of limp carcass down the driveway. A perfectly soiled trail of blood followed behind the body as if rolling out a red carpet. The deceased enemy's head, slumped down each step, receding from the driveway and into the street.

Moke picked up the AK that was lying next to the dead guy. He thought that Wildo had shot him from across the street, and he was already dying, just trying to hold out for one last shot on a Marine. His curly brown hair was matted down. His eyes were hazel green, already glazed over with that soullessness of death. He wasn't in Heaven, fucking 79 virgins; he was just splayed out, bleeding all 5.5 liters of his blood onto a random street with no name.

Moke pulled out the banana clip from the AK-47, cleared the rusty weapon, and tossed it down the street in a fit of rage. With a curious compulsion, he put his rifle inches from the deceased man's head and pulled off a shot. His cranium "popped" open like cracking a walnut, and then like deflating a basketball as it shriveled down in size, releasing a puff of pressure and air. His brain just kind of slid out of its cavity in a flow of bodily fluids. It was the first time he had seen anything like that. The blood splattered up the left side of his leg and pieces of brain matter were stuck in the compensator of his rifle.

The Battalion Commander, Mad Mike, appeared from out of nowhere like an apparition. Biting down on a cigar in his mouth, he walked alone down the street with his sidearm still in the holster and puffs of smoke billowing from behind him. He looked over at the explicit scene and smirked. "Well", he said, "it looks like we're doing some good work here today....carry on gentlemen". As if anything could ever be more "ungentle" of a man, an oxymoron, to say the least. However, there was still the matter of avenging Blanton, and ridding the target house of any live bodies.

It was four hours into the fight that day, and still, the enemy stubbornly remained cornered and defiant. After going from top to bottom, and nearly escaping a close encounter with insurgents from the rooftop stairway, First Squad had regrouped on the ground level. The house appeared to have been sufficiently suppressed with the amount of rockets and machine guns fired into it. Malik, as usual, felt compelled to take the lead on the most dangerous of missions. As the squad's point man, he was small in stature, merely a 5 foot frame. It actually looked quite ridiculous to see him geared up, because almost none of the standard military equipment fit him. His helmet was the smallest size that the government issued, and still it was too big for his head.

Growing up in Islamic East Africa, Malik was one of 13 children who immigrated with his family to the US as a teenager. Coming from a proud yet contentious heritage, his parents and family knew he was deployed abroad with the Marine Corps, but had no idea he was fighting in actual combat operations in Iraq. He managed to omit that part when sending phone calls and letters home. Being Muslim, he was revered among his peers for tactfully executing the distinction between "duty and faith". His duty and loyalty in protecting and fighting for the Marines against Islamic radicals was coupled with the enormity of being devoted to his faith in Islam. It was a tremendous undertaking for the soul. His moral and physical example of bravery was a testament of immense character.

Stacking along the wall with Malik was Fish, BS, Cherokee, Bull, and Bean Stalk. This time they made entry into the only other available point...the front doorway. The door had already been blown off. Much of the view from that point had been obscured with rubble and debris. After a few seconds creeping along the wall, Malik rushed in ahead of the others and jumped into a corner to the left, near the collapsed stairway. Immediately he was greeted by gunfire from the back of house. Then BS made entry as well with his SAW in hand, and he is met with another barrage as he dove onto the other side of another wall near the doorway. Now the two were effectively trapped, and the other Marines couldn't return fire or they would be firing directly at the Marines inside. The others were still stacked on the wall, trying to gain some type of initiative in fire superiority, but it was nearly impossible given the dug in angle of the insurgent's position.

It became quite a precarious situation for Malik. He hunkered behind a wall, and the insurgents were yelling at him, shouting indistinct chatter. He's called out to

BS to get out. Malik pulled the pin on a grenade and tossed it, as BS threw himself out the doorway. Then the insurgents kick the grenade back at Malik. He curled up small in a ball behind the wall. Boom!! The shock of the concussion rattled his insides, but he unflinchingly, prepped another grenade, pulled the pin, and held it, releasing the spoon. He counted, one-thousand, two...and threw it back.

After "cooking" the grenade, it exploded close to the insurgents as a shrilling scream of agony ensues, and he knew he hit one. Gunfire erupted mercilessly into Malik's position as the insurgents relented to giving up. Meanwhile, the rest of the squad is still on the wall, with no way to gain entry, the enemy had a bead on the doorway. The other guys outside could see Malik through a window encased in a steel grate, typical of the construction and security for houses in Fallujah. It's the only possible escape route for Malik to take. He almost surely would be killed if he tried to run back out the front door. And no one outside could give suppressive fire on the target because he could be shot by friendlies as well.

Immediately, Bean Stalk and his 250 lbs. of body began pulling the bars apart on the window so Malik could somehow squeeze through. They pulled and pulled and the others joined in. It looked similar to a jail break. Somehow, with all their strength, the Marines managed to bend the bars just enough that Malik could fit through with all of his gear still on. It was the most impressive thing to see. The feats that human beings can accomplish in desperate times are remarkable. Malik had just tossed the "hot potato" of grenades with insurgents. And then, with superhero strength, Bean Stalk pulled him out of an insanely, dangerous situation.

With both Malik and BS extracted from the house, the platoon brought another volley of intense gun and rocket fire down to bear. It was smoking and dusty inside the embattled structure, but the enemy was determined to answer back with a pop shot or two. They had to be low on ammunition, and the Marines had an unlimited supply. They were easily reinforced when an AmTrac rolled up on scene to resupply more ammo, grenades, and rockets. That was the mission for the rest of the day, to stay and eliminate the enemy until they were dead.

After making two attempts to enter the house and confront the enemy insurgents, it was futile to risk the lives of any more Marines. Probably one of the best decisions made the whole day, but there was no available air power, and it was still too close to execute a fire mission, because of the amount of friendlies in the area. The Marines had them cordoned off, cornered, they were bleeding, tired, out of ammo and water; it was only a matter of time before this standoff would cease. It was already late in the afternoon.

As the Marines from First Platoon occupied their positions, a few hours passed and there was no sound or movement from inside. Finally, after several requests for tank support, an M1 Abram tank arrived from across the open field. Like an eerie, imposing iron menace, it clanked slowly across the hard packed sand with welcomed hoots and shouts from the rooftops. "Oh they're fucked now", as the word buzzed around the squads. They emboldened the Marines with their presence, as its turret traversed the landscape, making a whining sound from the jet propulsion of her engine.

The guys operating the tanks were like saints to the grunts. The Marines of Fallujah didn't have that same affinity for anyone else, except CAAT and the AAVs. The utter elation expressed in their company was unparalleled. Marines getting all giddy and shit, like playing with their favorite toy. The tank commander lieutenant popped out from the hatch, conversing with some of the platoon leadership, getting oriented on direction and the overall scenario.

Immediately, they went to work loading tank round after tank round. They were firing into the house in such close proximity, merely 15-20 feet away from the target. All the grunts were standing right next to the tank, whilst punched by the concussion, as each volley of the main gun penetrated the house, blowing a backlash of debris and fire out the other side. After about six high explosive tank rounds were fired, the house began to collapse, as the roof tipped to one side and a few small fires burned inside. After the dust had settled, it was over.

The sheer concussion of the exploding tank rounds had directly contributed to killing the four insurgents that remained entrenched. Three of enemy fighters were pulled out, while another remained buried under the piles of concrete with one of his feet protruding out from underneath. Their faces were unrecognizable. One had a beard and was kind of chubby. The others face was gone and huge portion of his torso were gutted around mid-chest. The third insurgent, had his lower leg completely severed. Their bodies covered in soot and the blood strangely coagulated around their wounds. Their wounds didn't ooze blood. There were dead, so all functioning just stopped. They rolled them over checking their bodies. One of them had excrement soiling his backside. It produced some curious thought. Did he shit his pants before he died, or is that the body's natural, involuntary reaction to death? They kicked the dead enemy fighters around and spit on them. Just seemed like a natural reaction. They had avenged Blanton, but it couldn't be a celebration. They were all still in shock. They didn't have any time to actually process what had happened. Some used the tips of their boots to open the mouths of the dead, turning their heads, and investigating the parts of their contorted bodies.

The tanks remained, looming outside into the dusk, conversing with the grunts, beleaguered and proud of the work that they had helped trophy. The sun began to set that day and 7 bodies of enemy dead lay in the street, including the old man still on the rooftop patio. It was another exhausting day for First Platoon, especially First Squad, who had gallantly led the charge in retribution for their fallen comrade.

For his heroic and selfless action as the lead, point man of his squad in several heavy and chaotic, fire engagements, Malik was awarded the Navy and Marine Corps Commendation Medal with Valor.

Later that evening, they bedded down in the house across the street from where the corpses laid. The dogs came wandering in the night and made quick work of the easiest pieces of flesh on their faces. The night always accompanied a frigid blanket of air and ghostly hallucinations, remnants of the day's work. It invoked profound, individual reflection despite the brief respite from the madness outside.

Waking up in someone else's bed was weird, like an uncomfortably lucid experience. There is no way to cultivate the REM induced-coma needed to revitalized the senses, only being awake for a few hours with eyes closed, with other people's pillows and sheets still on the bed. Pictures of the family who dwelled there and ultimately fled, were randomly transfixed on the bedside tables. The sun had yet to crest, complete darkness and pungent human odors engulfed the bedroom.

At 0530...It was dark as fuck. Charlie is on the move early that next morning. They exited the house in a staggered column moving North, past the row of silhouetted mounds, unmoved since the day before. It left an impression on many of them, the ominous routine confirmed by the ghastly reality of grunt life, truly hardcore. They grew up watching war movies and glorifying heroes in battle, desperate to be tested. Now walking the embattled landscape, eyes told a different story. They were the movie. It was surreal. At certain points, cognitive retrospection catches up with what they actually saw or witnessed. It's just like "Whoa"..."Did I really just see that"? A lucid dream was a lucid nightmare. But they don't want to wake up. Just get it over with and let it play out because someone has to be next. It's a lottery. The odds are high. It's not the kind of gamble to be a millionaire. It's a gamble to live or die. But they all played...every day.

December 13, 2004 Charlie Co. 1/3

That day, they patrolled into the mid afternoon sun, finishing the clearing operation around a cluster of gutted out buildings near the Water Tower. It was a really good terrain feature in terms of figuring out where you were in the city at any given time. Similar to the way a grunt can reference the direction of the sun simply by knowing that it rises in the East and sets in the West. Wherever they were they could look to the city skyline and gauge their position, a useful tool when operating in the densely structured, residential areas.

The platoon was tasked with an overnight observation mission and set up blocking positions at key points around the vicinity of the FB Pickering. The individual fire teams would go out and bed down outside the wire of the firm base to have an effective presence and encounter enemy movement. Despite the Marine's NVG capabilities, most of the units were ill equipped to fight at night. Those were the days when Marines had to buy a lot of their own gear in terms of comfortability and efficiency, before M16s came with rail systems for mounting flashlights, and cool little accessories that could be added to increase the average grunt's advantage on the battlefield. Some guys would just buy their own tac lights and McGyver them to their weapon and gear. The "gear gurus" were the impeccable types that pioneered a lot of the current modern gear, known as a kit, or a load bearing, fighting vest, which allows for greater overall performance in combat.

In 2004, the reliability of NVG was more effective for stationary positions. The ill fitted gear and head mounts were cumbersome and ineffective, with early modeled equipment. At least that is how it is in the Marine Corps. The US Army is another story. The Marines usually relied on their own natural, night vision for any missions at night. The teams departed the firm base late in the afternoon. Each was tasked to set up in specific positions around the Water Tower. Cowboy was really paranoid for this mission because he was set to EAS within weeks. (End of Active Service), meaning he was getting out of the Marine Corps in less than a month. Meaning he was short. Foster and Moke drove the Humvees around running supplies back and forth.

It was no secret where they were positioned. Most of time, urban grunt operations are extremely overt in terms of what they are doing. It was a show of presence, while provoking the enemy to attack them essentially. That way, the infantry can do what they are made to do...identify, close with and destroy the enemy. It sounds ludicrous to most people when they really understand what a grunt does for a living. They pick fights. Whether the enemy is conventional or not is irrelevant, the tactics are still the same; to entice a confrontation with them, to overwhelm them with firepower, and to have a clear opportunity to destroy them. The Muj would pop up at certain times on a rooftop and fire off a few shots at the Humvees driving by. The Marines would return fire in that direction and it would stop, mainly harassing fires. The reality was always constant. They sought martyrdom. They wanted to draw the Marines in on their terms. The enemy wanted the Marines to pursue and chase them without a clear picture of the area and terrain. Meanwhile they are running from one mouse hole to the next, setting up to get the Marines in their trap, to try to equal the odds.

The enemy was growing impatient, an advantage to Marine operations if executed properly. Wildo and Pepe were getting shot at from some random sniper during their stint on the blocking positions. They joked about how terrible of a shot he was. The thought of chasing down solo artists was pointless. In that stage of the battle, it was more about life preservation. That "hero, Ooh-rah rah shit" was only reserved for a select few who really lived it, but the average Marine new this fight was over. There wasn't any point in dying in that shithole. Just do the job, get the mission done, and don't take unnecessary risks for a lone, forsaken wannabe martyr.

Squad leaders and team leaders carried the burden of losing any of their Marines. It's ultimately their responsibility to ensure their men stay alive and don't do anything stupid to get killed. They needed to focus on operating as safely as possible. As time crept closer to leaving Fallujah, the anxiety level surged. It's called "being short", and nobody wants to get hit so close to going home. It's a phenomenon that occurs every cycle of a combat tour.

They drove the Humvees, ripping through the mud puddles and over curbs. Switching up the route and driving down narrow streets at a high rate of speed. There is always that chance of a lucky RPG. Pedal to the metal, testing the complete range of the Humvees capabilities. It turned out to be pretty durable and reliable. They were put through hell, and even the high backs with zero up-armor held their own.

The patrols around the Water Tower continued every day, the days had been quieter with fewer contacts with the enemy, inevitably producing the dreadful complacency that ensues. The stench from the rotting bodies in stagnant water near the disabled aqueduct was nauseating; a whiff of the air riding a cool breeze with cold death and creepy skin. The hairs would stand up on their bodies, touching the fabric of their cammies, whilst pushing up goose bumps. The smell of death lingers in the mind thereafter as they pushed through the last houses on the block in the southern sector of the city.

The houses were spread more sparsely apart with openness in between. Half the houses were only partially constructed, low income households with meager accommodations, just a kitchen and a few rooms. In one of the rooms, a small black puppy was barely alive. It moved slowly, trying to pick up its head and stand on his feet. Severely weak from malnourishment and a terrible skin infection plagued his body with open sores. Ironically, he was lying atop a mound of discarded MREs, probably left from other units who had been through that area before. One of the Marines opened a pouch of beef stew, pouring some out for it to eat. The puppy was too weak to move, and stumbled to its feet. It walked a few steps, wobbling, and fell, too weak to eat. It couldn't have been more than a two months old and was probably born right around the time of the November invasion of the city.

It tugged at a few heart strings, even in the face of these hard charging, life taking Marines. A sick, dying puppy invokes their morality. Killing people doesn't do that, but poor little puppies will crush a man's sensibilities. They shot the puppy in the head with a 9mm pistol from the Corpsman. They did him a favor. It was the only compassionate thing left to do. That day they halted at Phase Line Honolulu, the southern boundary of their AO.

"Every Day Fallujah"

Pardon thee as we burst into flames
The AKs and RPGs are calling our names
Open your eyes and witness what they see
An ominous landscape of never-ending calamity
This place is poisoned, rotting from inside
A fanatical ideology from which no one can hide
Born into a side, hold on for the ride
Material has degraded to its truest form
Reality is weathered by the torrential storm
Structures fall to rubble, the hair on their face begins to stubble
When hagi comes to play, there is gonna be trouble
Put a round into his head and bust his bubble
Inhaling cigarette smoke and Composition B
No laws, no remorse, nor morality
Our habits are destructive, deliberately
Caught in the perils of the fight to be free
Look through a different pair of lenses to see
There is no life without the possibility of opportunity
All that remains are the instinctive survivors
The swift, elusive, terrorist connivers
Dogs and cats eating human cadavers
The evil city of hell on the Euphrates
No coins for enemy eyes while crossing the Hades
The crescent of a once thriving, fertile land

Damned to the cold, darkness, dust, and sand.

December 23, 2004...Charlie Co. Third Platoon, First Squad

Late in the afternoon, a small insurgent cell of activity opened up on FB Pickering by firing a few RPGs that hit the Hesco barriers surrounding the bunkered Marine position and some medium machine gun fire coming from the southwest of the firm base. The 240 machine gunners immediately returned fire, killing two of the enemy by initially having a complete and accurate vantage point to where the fire was coming from. The 51's also fired a few SMAW rockets into the target house. The CO (Commanding Officer) of Charlie Company was formulating a response to the audacious attack.

Meanwhile, there was chatter around the table as Wolverine's squad argued over a game of spades. They were called Third Herd, the biggest platoon in the entire company. They were some salty crusted-ass, sour mother fuckers. Just fuckin' grimy to tooth and nail. These were the guys no one wanted to fuck with, like a pack of jackals. It was best to just let them specialize in chaos and mayhem.

"Alright you guys, if the CO picks us to go raid that fuckin' house...we're goin", said Wolverine, stocky, muscular and symmetrical. He was the quintessential infantry leader, an All-American patriot. He was well respected amongst the company, especially within his platoon, but even they thought he was way too motivated and gung-ho. He didn't try to be a hero, he just naturally exhibited the warrior mentality. He had the frame of a lumberjack, and oddly enough, he hailed from a distinguished line of Ax Men and fire fighters in the industrious forest region of Northern California.

"Ahhhh, man! Fuck that bro! What the fuck? Why you always gotta fuckin' volunteer us"?!! Snarls and jeers backlashed from the squad. "Because, that's what we do" Wolverine exclaimed! "Shut the fuck up...if we get the word, we're going....gear up."

They grudgingly threw down the sets of cards in their hands and took a last swig from a warm, Iraqi cola. Lighting up their last cigarettes, their minds started to race because they knew they would encounter a close quarter fight. This wasn't going to be a surprise on a random clearing operation. It was a hunt to kill mission. The most savage type of engagement there is. They already knew where the insurgents were. He put in the request to volunteer his squad to go, and Captain Quiet obliged his initiative.

Third Platoon, First Squad stepped off, out the wire, to the South, enveloping a row of houses just a few blocks over from FB Pickering. Wolverine led his squad to the target house, and they split up the teams to make entry. Hot Sauce and Grimy maneuvered their teams from the bottom level, as they assaulted the house assertively, yet cautiously. Hot Sauce's team secured the bottom level. Grimy's team had cordoned the outside. The insurgents could hear their voices coming up. Hot Sauce's team got to the stairwell, ascending to clear the second level with Animal Mother rocking the SAW.

Animal was a salty ass, leviathan of a man at 6'5, with 260 lbs of grit and attitude. Once on the second deck, he crept quietly with Hops, a tenacious razorback from Arkansas who was dwarfed next to Animal Mother. Hops had already been wounded a few weeks before from some shrapnel in a fierce engagement with the enemy. He was now back in the rifle lineup and eager to get in the thick of it with his squad mates. His attitude was virtually fearless.

Suddenly, as they step into the center of the open room and pied off to the right, a huge man jumped out from behind a bathroom wall and grabbed a hold of Animal Mother with a grenade in his hands and a vest strapped to his chest. The attacking insurgent, also nearly the same height as Animal and easily over 200 lbs. he was momentarily stunned at the size of the Marine that he decided to lock onto. Hops started yelling "grenade" and everyone from Hot Sauce's fire team dove for cover and braced for the inevitable. Simultaneously, Animal Mother reacted instinctively by a natural inclination. He firmly held tight of his weapon as the insurgent attempted to bear-hug him. As in a textbook training manual, Animal Mother rolled and shifted his momentum, shaking the man from his grasp, repelled the attacker by using his weapon as leverage against him, pushing the enemy attacker back, while emptying a long burst of gunfire into the grenade wielding, suicide bomber .

It was almost in slow motion. The grenade fell from the insurgent's hand, he spun around, and the bullets from Animal's SAW gyrated through the enemies' flesh as it passed out of him to the other side. Just as everyone dived out of the way for cover, the enemy fighter and the grenade exploded, peppering Hops and Animal Mother in the legs, buttocks, and lower back. Wolverine, who was next in the stack, also caught some shrapnel to his face.

The insurgent was flat against the wall near the bathroom riddled with holes in his torso and face. His nerves were still twitching in an already dead body. As Animal Mother was shooting him, he was intensely focused on holding down the trigger at his target. He slowly walked backwards, until he felt a wall before diving to the ground in a perfect little corner. He crouched down as small as his disproportionately large body could get, with spots of blood wetting his cammies. He didn't know if it was his blood or someone else's. Concurrently, from behind the stairwell on the other side of the room, there some subtle movement from behind a blanket. It was another enemy who was wounded and hiding. Hot Sauce stepped over top of him and ended the Muj's silent quivering with few bursts to the chest, then motionless and listless. Animal Mother quickly ripped off the old plastic ammo drum, and replaced his SAW with a fresh 200 round package of goodness. His heart was pounding, and adrenaline pulsed through his veins. His mouth was dry and he swallowed to catch his breath. Animal was stunned amid the instant carnage, and how seemingly lucky he was.

Hot Sauce was yelling for a sit rep. It was loud and confusing. They were hollering back and forth at each other. Hops was wounded again, pulling himself down the stairs on his chest. Hot Sauce yelled to Animal, "Hey, come over to us". "Nah fuck you, you come to me", Animal reverberated back. It was so sudden they were expecting more enemy to pop out and they still didn't develop a clear picture to the situation. Hot Sauce was at the top of the stairway in front of a big open room leaning against a wall, alone, with Animal out of site. After a few minutes, Hot Sauce ran across the room and met up with Animal, internalizing every emotion, processing the fact that men were bleeding, and the house wasn't secure.

There was still another level to clear, and the uncertainty of any remaining enemy. Animal Mother and Hot Sauce stacked up with Wolverine. By this time, he was bleeding profusely from a gash on the side of his head, but he shrugged it off. They stacked back up and regrouped to finish the assault. After throwing to perfectly accurate grenades, they charged to the roof expecting to encounter more enemy. Instead, there lay two other dead insurgents with an empty RPG and medium machine nearby with a few hundred linked rounds. They "confirmed them" with a few shots each to the chest. They were the same guys that were firing RPGs at the firm base and the machine gunners waxed them with return fire before Wolverine's assault began.

During the ensuing melee above, Grimy's team shot up a third guy cordoned off on the bottom level as he jumped down from the roof and tried to escape. Wolverine then led another assault to the next house, but it was clear. That made five dead enemies for the day, and another three that were picked off by LAR nearby. That made eight enemy dead in total. Despite their superficial shrapnel wounds, it was another successful day for Third Platoon.

Wolverine's squad was beastly and that day just added to their reputation as marauding demagogues. It was a relief that the engagement was over, but they were mired in the shocking effect of surrealism. Animal Mother just stood there stoic, with his weapon resting on the wall, staring out over the city skyline. "Take a fuckin' picture man, I fuckin' wasted that dude". With blood stained cammies, he shook off his injuries and refused medical attention until later that night. Animal felt scorched with a newfound hatred and savageness that he'd never known, rambling on in muttered sentences, blasting aloud every explicit term in his vocabulary. He was the only one in Charlie Corps, perhaps the entire battalion, to actually engage in hand-to-hand combat with the enemy.

Hops was going off about how "he just came back from having lead in his ass and now getting it again". He joked about being a magnet. That would be Hops' second of three Purple Heart Awards during his tour in Iraq. Good natured and fiercely loyal, his squad mates revered his tenacity. He stubbornly cursed the insurgents despite his wounds, while the Corpsman worked to patch him back up, pleading to the doc not to MediVac him again. He was desperate to remain in the fight with his brothers.

December 12-23, 2004 Askari District....Kilo Co. 3/5

The last two weeks of December 2004 changed the scope of the battle. Darkhorse Battalion 3/5 had been ordered to stretch their AO to the East to include the Askari District. After Battalion 1/8 was removed from the city, The Lava Dawgs of 1/3 moved South of Highway 10 (PL Fran) to replace them in force, assuming control of 1/8's AO, from Queens to the Industrial District. As a result, 3/5 assumed control of 1/3's former AO in the Askari. It would prove to be the bloodiest fight yet for the Darkhorse Battalion 3/5.

The Askari District's rectangle-shape was the northeastern corner of the city. It was an affluent neighborhood by Iraqi standards. Impressive, well built, and storied dwellings decorated by artistic tiling on the walls and rot iron gates. It included many homes of former Baath Party officials, who had sympathies with the Sunni insurgency. It was also used as major point of operation during "pre-invasion" Fallujah, because of its close proximity to the Clover Leaf, which bisected the highways near the city, and led 40 miles east to Baghdad. It was a main artery, ripe with ambushes and mortar attacks. The Askari District also encompassed the Red Crescent Hospital and Janabi Mosque, which were both instrumental in aiding the insurgency in Fallujah. The Lava Dawg Battalion 1/3 led by Lieutenant Colonel Mad Mike had operated in Askari for over a month since the initial invasion. It was the scene of countless house to house engagements, firefights, and weapon caches. It was also the same area where, Medal of Honor nominee, Sgt. Peralta died, including a significant number of wounded and killed throughout the rifle companies of Alpha, Bravo and Charlie. When the 3/5 Battalion commander came over to meet with the commander of 1/3, Mad Mike confidently assured him that the Askari AO was completely cleared of insurgent activity.

After a few days from assuming command of re-clearing operations in the Askari, Kilo 3/5 became engaged in a huge firefight when they came upon a platoon sized element of enemy fighters holed up in a group of houses near Bravo Co.1/3's former firm base. Immediately upon taking fire, the Kilo Marines assaulted the buildings from top to bottom, using ladders they acquired from a nearby construction shop and jumping the gaps from roof to roof. After several Marines were killed or wounded while clearing the rooms, several more were wounded when they made further attempts each time to rescue their fallen comrades stranded in the houses.

The bitter, bloody engagement ensued for three days before the area was eventually demolished from dropping 500 lbs bombs during "danger-close" air strikes, virtually leveling the enemy position on block 915. In the days fighting from December 12-14, Kilo 3/5 lost five Marines killed in action and suffered over two dozen wounded, but killed over thirty enemy fighters. They also found the largest cache of the battle near the Janabi Mosque, which contained ammunition, rockets, and mortars that were stacked high from wall to ceiling. Pockets of resistance and small cells continued to pop up to kill and wound more Marines until the last major fighting ceased after December 23.

The heroic fighting of Dark Horse 3/5 has been well documented in other books and chronicles of history regarding the Second Battle of Fallujah. In the last few weeks of December 2004 alone, Battalion 3/5 was awarded with countless individual acts of courage and sacrifice, including 4 Navy Cross and 2 Silver Star Citations (the 2nd and 3rd highest awards for bravery) for gallantry and intrepidity during combat operations within the city.

Other sources of literature have documented the efforts of the four, Marine Infantry Battalions involved in Operation Phantom Fury, but credit 1/3's involvement in the battle as "less than remarkable". As an outsider to the "Good, Old Boy Network" and coupled with his Pentagon affiliations, Mad Mike was ostracized by his peers within the officer community. After-action reports by the other battalion commanders participating in Phantom Fury inevitably charged Mad Mike and his Hawaii Marines as being culpable and negligent in their methodology while conducting clearing operations within the Askari District. With that being said, the politics within the officer corps turned the affair into a pissing contest. Some of them held the Lava Dawgs indirectly responsible for the casualties suffered by the Dark Horse Marines. Despite the finger pointing, the twelve days before Christmas in Fallujah proved the elusive strategy and fanaticism of the enemy fighters to be a tough, battle of attrition for the grunts on the ground. "All gave some, some gave all".

Chapter 9
Clearing and Caches

Late December 2004

First Platoon, Charlie Company continued to spread out their fire teams and set up blocking positions near the Water Tower. It was a unique experience because it gave the small teams of three or four Marines the opportunity to operate with some relative autonomy. Marines operated more effectively in smaller more manageable units and were taught to fight that way. Weed's team departed FB Pickering and set up a blocking position in a bomb crater near the middle of the street. The crater was about 3 feet deep, and they utilized chunks of concrete to extend the cover around their position. However, when they began receiving sniper fire from the rooftops, they chose to move their position to a location offering more overhead cover.

After clearing a nearby house, Weed began booby trapping their position. He exuded industrious and creative qualities, and did so calmly and confidently. Weed had really evolved into a natural warrior. Growing up shooting, hunting, and fishing in Idaho, he learned to excel at the Art of War and how to create innovative and useful tools to benefit the unit. The dry desolate environment did not confuse his instincts in the least. He could put things together with some dental floss and duct tape, while picking a guy off from 500 yards with pinpoint accuracy. After setting up a few flares and grenades, the Charlie Marines finally stopped to rest atop a pile of cinder blocks and dug into their MREs. It was a quiet, cold, windless night. As they ate, a single rock fell from a hole in the roof. Then, more silence, and eerie occurrences like the rock. They cleared the house again to the roof, and nothing.

A few days later, the platoon operated near FB Pickering, as Christmas quickly approached. The Marines looked forward to the holiday because Command scheduled them to rotate back to Camp Fallujah for 24 hours. Once there, they would prioritize their time, focusing on showers, a good night's sleep on a cot, a PX run, and a mandatory haircut, in that order. Trying to keep the guys focused proved difficult, due to the monotony of clearing houses. Complacency resulted from the much anticipated R & R, as daydreams about taking a shit in a real toilet danced in their heads. As they progressed through one particular block, they encountered sporadic sniper fire, near a large open soccer field and playground featuring a rusty jungle gym. Duffy, the company clerk, sustained a bullet wound to the foot.

In response, the SMAW teams fired several rockets in the general vicinity of the sniper, blowing a hole in the side of the building and window. The whole platoon scrambled and lunged behind a wall. They immediately entered the corner house and began clearing in order to get a rooftop vantage point, and returned fire. The M203 gunners repeatedly lobbed 40 mm grenades across the field to their max effective range of 400 meters. Aimed at a 50 or 60-degree angle, the grenades flew high into the air with a loud "thump," until a puff of black smoke and a delayed explosion signaled the impact. That day ended like many others, with harassing fires attempting to entice the Marines to pursue. The Marines did not oblige the enemy, maintaining their professional bearing. Ideally, when facing harassing fire, they would employ overwhelming firepower from a relatively safe distance. Of course, the insurgents wanted to narrow that distance down to inches instead of meters. If an insurgent happened to escape, the Marines would simply mow them down. Open areas afforded the opportunity to max out the effective range of their weaponry and hurt the enemy with precision. If a tank – or air support – was available, the firefights usually ended much sooner.

Minutes later, a loud "Swoosh" passed high overhead. The Marines quickly caught a glimpse of a friendly bomb plummeting from the sky. "BOOOOOM"! The bomb impacted directly on top of the building, launching dirt and rock hundreds of feet into the air. A half second later, the Marines felt the powerful explosion, as the concussion caught up with the speed of the sound. The power of such force amazed the Marines. It was exhilarating and humbling at the same time. American air power made the most dangerous and committed fighters simply disappear into vapor and dust. It was impressive to say the least, and a wonder why the opportunity for the use of air assets was not afforded more frequently. Collateral damage was usually cited as a reason to employ Marines into buildings over a disproportionate use of air power to exterminate a threat. In those moments, they were reminded of their expendability. Lives were traded in lieu of discretion. But in this case, it was a good day to have "air".

The Marines paused in the courtyard of the house, as the Charlie Company leadership assessed the damage and reported back to the Battalion Commander, Mad Mike, a.k.a. "Bronco 6." They prepared to regroup and push back to the firm base. While patrolling down the street in a column, Napoleon walked vigilantly next to Moke. Napoleon looked over at a locked aluminum shed. It looked suspicious, because anything with a lock on it was usually broken off and investigated. It just looked odd, too blatant. Napoleon yelled out, "Lock!" He walked over in order to investigate. "Hey man, we need to blow this and check it out, it could be a cache," Napoleon advised. Moke looked over at him, puzzled and irritated. They were on their way back for some rest and chow, so he did not express support for the idea. It would require time to set up the detonation cord and blow it, and they did not have bolt cutters. And if they found anything, they would need to spend hours conducting an inventory of the suspected cache.

Nonetheless, Moke understood Napoleon's view. It would be irresponsible to leave a suspected cache in the hands of the enemy, only to be used against Marines. Torn between a selfish tick and his duty, Moke acquiesced. "Ahhhhh, what? Man, you just want to set off more demo," Moke exclaimed. "I'm serious, we have to check this out, there could be a bunch of shit in there," replied Napoleon, convincing his comrade. Moke took his helmet off, and huffed a bit, shook his head. "How much time to set up"? "Two minutes", hurried Napoleon. Moke yelled to halt the squad. "Possible cache....hold up and set security", he yelled down the road to the others. They didn't mutter a word, just took a knee. A tank pulled up, randomly. Malik took the opportunity to converse with the tankers, and take a few pictures with the crew chiefs helmet on. The tanks were an awesome sight, and of course everyone felt invincible with them around.

Napoleon finished taping up the detonation cord that ran to some C4, fitted with a blasting cap set for 1 minute. Everyone cleared out of the way and he yelled out the countdown (as he always did) in the remaining 5 seconds. Boom! He didn't set it to be a powerful blast, just enough to blow the lock off. The demo punched a whole into the flimsy, roll-up aluminum door. They pulled it aside, and crouched to walk underneath. It was just a small garage, type shed with some construction tools and an industrial (Dewalt) stationary saw. It looked like a good piece of equipment, but nothing else cluttered the shed, which was odd because they were usually packed full of storage. Behind the equipment was a thin piece of plywood, applied in a rudimentary construction, but precisely nailed off. Everything just looked too neat and tidy. As Moke looked closer it looked like they could just rip it down from the frame. Before doing so, he foolishly fired a few rounds into the wood at chest level. For some reason, he felt like someone might be in there, hiding. Then he slowly reached to the corner of the wood, pulled gently, and just popped the nail out. And then pulling some more, and another nail popped open, before the entire piece of plywood came tearing down, exposing a sizable weapons cache.

All the Marines yelled in celebration when it was found, and Moke had to recant his cynicism and credit Napoleon with a job well done. The cache consisted of 4 RPKs, 2 PKMs cleaned and oiled, several types of small arms of some American M16s, AKs and RPGs with thousands of rounds of ammunition, hundreds of mortar rounds marked in crates from Syria, det cord, explosive material for making IEDs, and one large 155mm artillery shell. It was a hell of a find. Each time a cache was confiscated, several lives were saved as a direct result. Napoleon, a salty ass PFC (Private First Class), the second lowest enlisted rank, was the assault section leader because he really knew his shit with demolitions. The guy who officers scoffed at, who was busted down twice in rank for insubordinate conduct, was the hero of the day.

Back at FB Pickering, things were starting to revert back to the usual "garrison" bullshit. The tempo started to slow down a bit and the SNCOs use the time to enforce every MAR ADMIN on the books, regulations that guided hygiene standards and appearance, like fresh rank insignias and bloused boots. There were hundreds, if not thousands of known guidelines of what is or what is not authorized. The Marines definitely no longer got away with a 5 o'clock shadow on their faces, sometimes overlooked during the heavier weeks of fighting. Every time a Marine had to shit, eat, or brush his teeth...there were specifics to engaging in such activity. There was always a designated area. Understandably so, there had to be. 150 Marines excreting bodily fluids on a daily basis tends to add up with infectious and fetid human waste. Obviously to most homo sapiens, they don't want to "shit where they eat", so to speak.

So, the burn pit was to the rear corner of the FB, wash area was on the opposite side, and the mortar pit was in the middle of everything. It was just another random happening. Not to mention, every time you went to these designated places to do the business at hand, it was out in the open, with no cover or concealment. So of course, they had to go with all their gear and their weapon, just in case something popped off, or a sniper was taking shots. Try taking a shit with flak and kevlar in a 100 degree heat in a small, smelly tent-like apparatus. It's been done...many times. The hardest part is the wipe after. Then, the burn pit was a hop, skip, and a throw, where some unlucky boot bastard would be there skimming away, and tending to the odoriferous brew. After laughing at how bad his life sucked, a walk on to the next designated area for a tooth brushing. Promptly pulling out an antibacterial baby wipe for good measure and wipe those hands down thoroughly, lest some residue from the ass wipe still remain. Most times, one would prefer to brush their teeth before wiping their ass, but shit happens. Marine grunts are experts at living in these conditions, they not only endured it, they embraced the "SUCK" of it. It's a fuckin' badge of honor. Some guys thought it was a record that they went 38 days without a shower. And it was if they never entered into that territory, where they existed within a few layers of crusty, dirty, salty, grime. Baby Wipes were their only salvation. It seemed too primitive that human beings could even survive that long without a shower. Americans take at least 1-3 a day, back home. This shit is deep....talking about monthly showers, maybe. Then the guys who went six months without a shower, still in the same pair of cammies, so stiff they were like sand paper, and stuck out on some remote outpost in Afghanistan are cursing you for being a pussy. It was all relative, most grunts on the line were getting at least one shower a month. There is always some asshole, hard-ass who has legitimately had it tougher for lack of whatever. But relatively speaking, during the four month mission in Fallujah, they might have been blessed with at least 4-5 showers.

Of course, all the esteemed support elements in the rear of the infantry, especially field grade officer types and Senior SNCOs, are almost certainly guaranteed at least one hot meal in the chow hall, a shower a day, and possibly even, a full night's sleep. Two of the simplest morale boosters in a combat environment are (1) the chance to take a shower in an actual shower and (2) take a shit in an actual toilet. A person would be surprised of how much that is taken for granted on a daily basis. It returns some sense of dignity back to being human, because grunts are essentially, part-time animals.

An Encounter with a Lava Dawg Sniper

The STA (Surveillance and Target Acquisition) team woke up early that morning near the Soda Factory at the eastern most VCP (Vehicle Check Point) into the city. It was a FB that mostly housed members of Weapons Company 1/3, like snipers and the CAAT teams, who were notorious for their "hell on wheels" approach to fire support. They were alternating their trucks for day and night missions, so the guys could get some much needed sleep. It was setting off to be a great morning for the unit because some of them were going back to Camp Fallujah for a brief 24 hour respite from the battle. They gathered up their gear with packs, including their Batman and Scooby Doo blankets, some good luck trinkets that they acquired along the way, and of course "the bag" that carried their scopes and the M24 sniper rifle.

They climbed into the back of a 7 ton for the ride out of the city. Just then, Sniper Doc spotted the lieutenant approaching them. "Watch this, LT is gonna tell us we have another mission". Merlin was sitting next to him, looking bamboozled in utter disbelief. "Hey, gents we need you to be the QRF (Quick Reaction Force) for LAR (Light-Armored Reconnaissance), who had been clearing a few houses to the North and got hit hard. Merlin just tightened his lips in disgust and gave Doc a soft jab to the chin. The 1/3 STA team was an elite group of the (03) grunts, the eyes and ears of the battalion. They are the violent, but silent professionals that can turn the tide of a battle with one shot or conduct a slew of improvisational missions as an effective and tactical, battalion asset.

As they set off on the patrol, word came over the radio that a Marine was trapped in the house they were en route to. As they turned the corner, the snipers witnessed the ensuing mayhem. Marines were running around amid the chaos, and screaming into the air, "I'm not going back in there"!, while Corpsman attended their wounds. A Major was standing there with his arms crossed. "Who here has cleared houses together"? The sniper team walked onto the scene, each with a hand up. "We have, sir", they replied and promptly volunteered themselves into the fray.

The LAR Marines, that the snipers rushed in to support, were clearing some houses when they were ambushed by a small cell in the upper level of the target house. The LAR unit had taken multiple casualties when they were hit, and one Marine was killed and left in the house as they proceeded to evacuate. Upon realizing their fallen brethren was missing, they organized a fire team to go back in to rescue him and they were all hit and wounded by enemy fire and grenades. Then they organized a squad sized element to re-assault the enemy fighters inside, and again they were repelled back, increasing the number of Marines wounded.

The STA team made a brief observation of the layout and coordinated their movement. The stack consisted of four of them, Sniper Doc, Merlin, Rick, and Styx. After an extended onslaught from the 240 machine guns from a support by fire position, the team made entry, with Merlin exalting an aggressive roar. Suppressing the upper windows of the house, emptying a magazine with his M-16, Doc covered their movement. Sniper Doc was a Navy Corpsman attached to the special unit of Marines, responsible for treating the wounded. However, in this case, Sniper Doc performed the dual function of a "trigger puller" as well. Highly revered among his fellow Marines, he was tenacious, not the typical Corpsman, hence his position within the STA team. They turned the corner of the house, stepping on all the broken glass, as a shots from AK fire rang out from inside.

Merlin immediately fell hard to the ground. They thought he was shot, but he just slipped on the glass fragments littering the floor. Merlin got up and they proceeded around a dark and smoky corner near the stairway, their vision obscured as a silhouette passed in the shadow. Styx jump in front of the stack, on point with a Mossberg, single barreled shotgun. With fierce momentum and intensity, Styx sensed movement and swung around the corner, blasting an insurgent on the stairway in the face, while racking the chamber of the shotgun and killing a second enemy behind him. With Doc in trace, he fired and killed a third fighter who was running to the next room. They accomplished this remarkable feat of MOUT (Military Operations in Urban Terrain) dominance while walking up a stairway, which is extremely difficult because the Marines were at a major disadvantage due to the nature of their position. They made it to the second level, cleared it, and retrieved the body of the dead Marine who was lying in the doorway of a room. Merlin was cursing, "You mutha fuckas"! A flood of emotion came over the snipers as they carried the body out into the street and removed his flak to check for any vital signs. Lance Cpl. Blake Magaoay, 20, from Pearl City, Hawaii, was gone. It was the first time Sniper Doc had ever taken someone's pulse, and didn't feel one.

For his heroic actions in killing two insurgents and helping to retrieve the body of a fallen Marine, Styx was awarded the Navy and Marine Corps Commendation Medal with Valor.

Chapter 10
A New Calendar

December 25, 2004

Christmas day came like any other. There was nothing special about it, other than the cognitively distorted images of family and friends back home, sitting around piles of empty boxes, discarded gift wrapping, and the smell of honey ham and baked goods. Snow probably graced the ground somewhere, and maybe a glint of sunlight peeked through the pines, illuminating crystallized snowflakes. The holidays would remain forever tainted for the young Marines. Someone created a song called "Christmas in Fallujah," but none of the Marines had heard it yet. But back home, it likely streamed through the airwaves and radios on American kitchen counters, back when the schmooze of the war still seemed a patriotic and worthy endeavor.

Mothers baked their son's favorite pecan pie, even though he wouldn't be there to enjoy it. Families gathered around recalling the yuletide. Many youngsters would be saying things like, "Mom, how did Santa get this down the chimney?" The Marines reflected on how they figured out Santa wasn't real, for instance when one came down the stairs in the middle of the night on Christmas eve, squeamish from anticipation, only to see Mom wrapping presents and organizing them under the tree. They all agreed that it wasn't an easy thing for their parents to explain away. Kids are innocent, because they trust wholeheartedly. They innately have faith in what they are told.

The OPs (Observation Posts)

After the platoons rotated back for a brief 24-hour R & R at Camp Fallujah, the mission began to change. Slowly, the city opened to the public through ECPs (entry control points), subject to an 1800 (6pm) curfew. Residents were provided identification cards and permitted to return to their obliterated homes. The damage shocked most of them. Few buildings escaped significant damage. The USMC's office of Public Affairs distributed flyers containing Arabic instructions on how to file a claim for damage. If the residents qualified, they would receive a fixed amount of a few thousand dollars for compensation. Some homeowners immediately began the arduous process of removing broken blocks of concrete, clearing debris, and reacquiring some semblance of home.

A minivan, what was left of it, was parked outside of a man's house. The man subordinately grinned as he inspected his bullet-ridden vehicle. It looked as if it had been hit with a tank round, and then run over by it. Upside down, half of one side completely flattened, and a front wheel exposed, raised into the air. The man tried to remain humble and friendly to the Marines patrolling the streets, brandishing their gear and weaponry. The Marines joked and mocked his misfortune on video. Apparently, the man still owned one good vehicle, which he drove back into the city with his brother-in-law, bullet holes in the windshield and all. The Iraqi man put his hand on the exploded vehicle's tire, rolling it around in circles, while smiling and giving the "thumbs up" sign. Then he exclaimed, "Boom! Good! America, good. Saddam, no good!" The Marines knew the man merely placated them, but still got a kick out of it. He did not claim a side. He was impartial. Both sides likely caused him to suffer at some point.

The Marines just kept filming and patronizing the returning residents with questions in English they didn't understand. Other civilians typically just squatted, in a cultural fashion, in front of the driveways along the street with stoic, aimless faces. The Marines did not feel sorry for them, nor did they feel they should. Before they fled, those residents likely aided the insurgents that killed their friends. Even if they didn't provide direct support to the enemy, most were guilty by association.

By this point, First Platoon constituted the lightest platoon in Charlie Company, in terms of the number of Marines able to fight. As such, Command ordered First Platoon to control a series of three OPs (Observation Posts) along Highway 10 (PL Fran). Second and Third Platoons continued the grueling work of re-clearing block after block and finding large caches along the way, almost daily. It actually became quite competitive between the lieutenants, for which platoon could find the largest cache. Some small, others extremely large, but the elusive enemy never seemed to be in short supply of options in terms of where to get a weapon. Before the battle, there were hundreds and thousands of caches stashed all over the place. They executed urban, guerilla tactics, similar to the way the VC used to hide weapons in heaps of rice in Vietnam.

The insurgency sometimes used entire living rooms and kitchens, small sheds, and holes in the ground with all sorts of innovative ways to hide or conceal them. Charlie Company accounted for the discovery of over 100 different caches of weapons and munitions ranging from every type and model, including US weaponry, and originating from every known enemy of the Western World. Stockpiles of confiscated weapons lay on the ground in the FB waiting to be destroyed. Many of them were rusted and seemingly inoperable due to wear and neglect. Cleanliness of a weapon tells many things. It shows discipline, careful thought, initiative, and preparedness. A Marine could immediately decipher many things just by looking at fine detail. Like a detective observes a crime scene, they see clues to the inevitable defeat of their enemy.

On December 26, First Platoon set off in the early morning as the call to prayer resumed due to all the civilian activity. The sun crested the tops of the minarets, as they patrolled past the Water Tower, down PL Ethan to the intersection of PL Fran. About a fifteen minute walk along the gravel filled roads that bordered homes to the West and the industrial shops to the East. They came to a corner building about seven stories tall. It was directly on the corner of Fran, opposite the only working gas station in the city. Surrounded by barbed wire and barricades, it reminded Groucho of a bombed out, version of the "Capital Records Building" in LA. Smaller in scale, it was more square than round, but seemed like an interesting first impression.

The bottom foundation had been half destroyed from the mechanized onslaught of the initial invasion months earlier. It was a wonder how stable the structure actually was from collapsing. The bottom two levels were gutted out with twisted metal framing, insulation, and drywall, exposing the concrete pillars that skeleton supported the building. There was only one entrance covered by a constructed metal gate, and a large steel plate 6x8 feet, weighing a few hundred pounds that they slid back and forth in front of the gate for extra security. A zigzagging stairwell led to each floor up to the top level and roof. Every level up to the 4th floor was unlivable, but the Marines bedded down on the sixth floor with orders to man the surrounding roof OPs, 24/7. Unbeknownst to their arrival to OP3, they would be sharing responsibilities with members of the largely Shiite and newly formed, Iraqi National Guard (ING).

They had been reconstructed and formed in response to the failure of the former "Fallujah Brigade", a sort of organized militia of mostly Sunni soldiers from Saddam's former Army that was backed up by the Americans, but proved to be deeply corrupted and sympathetic to the insurgency. Because of the sectarian rift between Sunni and Shiite Muslims, it was necessary to employ Shiite soldiers into the ING to lessen the likelihood of corruption that had plagued the Fallujah Brigade in the earlier months of 2004, which directly contributed to the failed attempt to pacify the city in April and free it of insurgent control. Many of the ING had only been in service a few months. Some were former soldiers who served in Saddam's Army, while many had virtually no experience in soldiering and were merely trying to have a job to send money home to their families.

There were three main OPs along 1/3's northern AO at strategic vantage points because of the main artery of traffic that ran right through the middle of Fallujah. To the South of Fran, it overlooked all of Queens. To the East, all the way down the long straight, Highway 10 was the Industrial District. To the West, down to the tip of the Pizza Slice and the Iraqi Police station was where Fish's Squad manned OP1, the limit of the AO. To the North of Fran was the Jolan and Askari Districts, Battalion 3/5's AO.

OP1 was roughly two decks high with a rooftop OP, overlooking a densely populated section near the Jolan, known for shoot outs and assassinations with the fallible Iraqi Police. The remaining Marines of Fish's squad operated it with a small contingent of ING. Each of the OPs served as a sort of cooperative test case between the American Marines and the ING a sign of solidarity between the two nations. Influencing the notion that the US were not occupiers, but instead liberators, and eventually transitioning the ING and the Iraqi Police to take full responsibility of their own security and stability. Effectively known as, democratization. First Squad was made up of Fish, Bull, Cherokee, Lanky, Malik, Beef, and BS. They worked well together. They were a salty, tight knit group after all they had been through in the previous months together. They had their squad leader and all the team leaders were still in the line, but they had no SAW gunners. Remy, Razor and Blade, the squads' only SAW gunners, had suffered serious wounds and never returned along with several others who were badly wounded like Harley, Skinny, and Doc B.

OP2 was manned by Wildo and JD's teams with Pepe, Merc, 8 Ball, and Shooter, from Second Squad. They were in another building several stories high, near a large mosque with tall minarets, proportionately distanced between the other two OPs which were spread out about a mile apart. Just close enough that their hand-held radios could still catch enough frequency to pass a message or a radio check. OP2's position near the mosque made for the most picturesque of daily sunsets, as the two audacious minarets captured the receding, yet a particularly foreboding, horizon with absolute symmetry.

OP3 was inhabited by the rest of Second Squad, consisting of Weed, Cowboy, Deuce, Groucho, and Moke. It was directly on the corner of Ethan and Fran, across from the gas station. It all just seemed shady as fuck. They just threw them out there to pull fire watch because someone had to do it. But it wasn't really a bad gig. It gave them a chance to rest a bit, operate under some relative autonomy, free from the constant scrutiny of regulations and shit like that back at FB Pickering. The fundamentals of infantry life always reverted back to small unit operations, and more often than not, if a 3-4 man fire team could click together, the missions would go off with minimal problems. It invokes an endearing term of "keeping things in-house", which affords the men the opportunity make decisions, be convenient, to hash out their own problems, issues, etc. amongst each other in terms of the operational tempo, without fear of the company "sprinkling ink" all over the place, a military term for describing any sort of punitive, administrative action for disobeying orders and regulations.

Initially, it took the Marines at the different OPs a little while to get used of the idea of sleeping and operating so close with the ING. After all, they were Iraqi, and still suspect. The Marines were obviously the mentors, but the ING were poorly trained, undisciplined, loud, and virtually impartial to the cause of the United States. They just wanted a job that would pay something to send to their families, and the only two jobs for hire in Fallujah were the US Government and Al-Qaeda. The Iraqis had different reasons for joining, but it was largely due to the politics of the country and their religious sect. Sunni and Shiite are rivals within the same religion, similar to Protestants vs. Catholics. Saddam was part of the ruling Sunni minority, which presided over a predominantly, Shiite Iraq. Fallujah was a Sunni city, so naturally the "Think-Tankers" needed to hire Shiite Muslims into the ING to avoid the greater chance for corruption and sympathetic infiltrators from the Sunni side.

The average ING had a low regard for basic things that Marines normally have "shit fits" about, like general discipline and weapons safety, for example. There is a specific protocol to handling a rifle as well as exhibiting professional conduct. It's well engraved in the Marine mindset. It's a miracle the ING didn't kill each other by their sheer aloofness. A negligent discharge from their weapons was a fairly, frequent occurrence. It was nerve racking to the Marines. The ING didn't really patrol too much, serving more as a glorified security guard force for US politicians and their "Dog and Pony Show". The Marines were leery of them, but attempted to assimilate and execute their orders, which were to maintain the OP to observe and disrupt enemy movement along Fran and support further operations within the AO.

The Marines and the ING each had their own side separated by the zigzagging staircase that split down the center of the building. As the days went by the men developed the "watch routine", around the clock, Marines operated one post for a set time and number of hours, and then an ING soldier operated the other post, rotating on a consistent and repeating basis. Each man would be relieved at the designated time by the next watchman. After finishing their duties on post, provided there were no patrols scheduled, the Marine would be free to sleep, read, eat, write, play cards, jerk off, take a shit, etc, within the confines of the OP. The posts were positioned in diagonal corners of the rooftop, surrounded by a wall of sandbags. They could see the whole city in any direction.

The ING soldiers seemed to be receptive to a rapport and revered the Marines, as the small detachment responded in kind. Sabaa, 24, from Mosul, was probably the best of the ING from a military perspective. He spoke the most English, some education, and was a former soldier in Saddam's Army. He was forced to join the army at 18. He claimed he had been a tank driver during the Invasion of Iraq in 2003. That he did not want to fight the Americans and that he and the other soldiers ran and abandoned their positions in the desert near Um-Qasr, when US forces crossed the border. In retribution for his mutiny upon returning home, loyalist thugs of the Baath Party killed both of his parents and he fled for his life. He still managed to have a smile on his face most days and remained enthusiastic about a better future.

Awar, 27 from Najaf, also said Saddam killed his parents, years before. He was good at "McGyvering" TVs and satellite dishes to pick up some Arabic television. They also had stacks of bootlegged CDs of American movies with the corniest B-rate, dubbed or subtitled dialogue. Playing music from an old Walkman rigged up to a small speaker emanating an eerie, trance-like Middle Eastern tune. The perpetual flute and mysticism always tweaked out the anxiety of Western sensibilities. They insisted the Marines were guests and to sit and drink some tea. For dinner they brought them their own styro-foam box of rice, chicken and lentils with a cucumber or a tomato. The Marines didn't expect such hospitality, but quickly realized it was better than MREs every day.

Fathal, 19, was the youngest, shortest, and most irresponsible of the bunch. He joked a lot and loved asking questions about America and looking at porn. They were instantly corrupted by the library of porn that the Marines toted around in their patrol packs. Porn magazines proved to be a bartered currency or powerful negotiating tool. Kalef, 19, from Nasariyah, laughed continuously and was rarely seen without a cigarette hanging from his mouth.

Lastly, there was Adil, 39, from Basra, the oldest and respected leader of the group, a devout Muslim and father of 5 children. They were innovative and enjoyed any relative comfort they could muster. It was customary for them to straddle each other, sitting on the floor with arms and legs wrapped together. The scene appeared especially homosexual, but apparently it was culturally platonic for men to engage in this way. The Marines just laughed and shook their heads, often retreating back to "their" side of the building. The smells, sounds, and sights were foreign. It was an unexpected culture shock for the bewildered Americans.

December 31, 2004

The eve of a New Year was closing in just a few hours away. It seemed surprisingly quiet and uneventful until H-hour, exactly 2400, on January 1, 2005. The sky exploded with bursts and screaming, streams of red and white star clusters, smoke flares, illumination parachutes, and a brief cyclic, cacophony of celebratory gunfire. Then, abruptly ending as quickly as it began, a bit of youthful exuberance to expel out the old and bring in the new. The displaced Fallujans were a bit perplexed at all the commotion. The Islamic calendar doesn't recognize the Western, Free World's beginning of a New Year on that day. The stagnant smoke lingered in the dense cold with no breeze to blow it along. New Year's Day in a combat zone; branded, embedded on the frontal lobe. Glad to see 2005. It's a miracle. Shivering and sitting in a plastic chair, eyes peeled and watery, staring out yonder into the darkness, the rooftops.

The Comet

During the night, the cold silence fell over a twinkled little sky. The air was calm with the frigid stillness that only deserts know. The stratosphere illuminated with a million sparkling specks and bursting supernovas. A dying star fell back to earth, like a fiery cannonball, disintegrating from its tail, a rapidly burning wick. His mind drifts far out into galaxies and back to little, tropical hot spots around the globe. He was interrupted by a distant burst from a 240, like a bad dream, jolted from serenity and jaded by the infantry. The hands strike the hour, counting down seconds to chime. Pushed so far fast forward, there is too much to rewind. The days dragged along in the race against time. From the rising sun, there is enough to get it done. Luminous shadows in the blink of an eye. Al-Fajr erased the night sky.

Shooting at Ghosts - January 6, 2005...OP3

After assuming the post at 2200 hours, Deuce was scanning the area with some outdated, bulky thermal imagery on his SAW, when he noticed several white silhouettes walking around a rooftop to the southwest of OP3's position about 150 meters away. He relayed down to the others who were milling about downstairs. Weed and Moke came jogging up the stairway to see what was going on. Deuce explained to them what he thought he saw, passing off the weapon to get a second view and opinion from the others. The thermal sight known as a "Starlight Scope" was designed to give off a heat signature, which is easy to see at night because the heated image is really white, while the surrounding environment is made up of cool, opaque shades of grays and black. However, it only offered the visual outline of something, not much detail other than a silhouette shape.

After each of them caught a minute to look through the sights, they all conferred that it appeared to be a group of men, walking, sitting, and leaning against the second story level of a house. In the typical fashion of many houses in Fallujah, the roof also served a dual purpose as a patio area. They looked, and looked, and watched the subjects casually roam about. Weed pulled out his NVGs to see if he could get some better clarity. It appeared to be about 6-8 males, with slung weapons, standing around. One was sitting, leaning against a wall. Another wall on the other side of the patio would obscure the view of them as they be-bopped to and fro. Moke got on the radio to confirm if there were any friendly OPs to their south or south west. Spartan 6 radioed back that there was an Iraqi National Guard post on the other side of PL Henry to their southwest, but that position had to be at least almost 800 meters to a full click away from OP3. The enemy suspects at the target house were much closer at about 300 to 400 meters away. From their vantage point, the target house was a few feet lower in respect to their view of the ING post. It was a bit odd because, the suspected enemy position was directly in line to the ING post, from the perspective of OP3. It was as if the suspects had set up in that location purposely to set up a cross fire between the ING post and OP3. It was puzzling, but it seemed like a clever maneuver on the part of the enemy.

The Marines continued to scan the area, monitor the situation, and switched back and forth every few minutes to try to come to an agreement on what they were seeing, while at the same time, keeping contact with the Spartan 6 back at the CP in FB Pickering. Was it a legit target or were they all just hallucinating? If it was in fact the ING post in their sights, they didn't place the distinguishable identifiers around their location, known as IR Fireflies, which were like strobe lights only viewable through NVGs. That alone would have ruled out any confusion of who was who or where. They continued, painstakingly to identify the target or any possible friendlies that were on a patrol in the area and there were no friendly patrols in the area.

Weed started marking the target with his PEQ-2s, which emits a laser, also only viewable through NVGs. Moke was on the radio with OP2 to get information of what they could see. Weed kept "painting' the house with the PEQs. OP2 said they could see the house they were "painting" and that the ING post was still several hundred meters to the West of where they were at OP2. They said they didn't have any thermal imagery because the batteries were dead, and what they could see with their NVGs was questionable because their vantage point was in defilade to the target house. It seemed obvious there was some trickery going on. Moke gave the go and Deuce opened fire with his SAW.

The target erupted and all the silhouettes scattered, two of them dropped to the ground near the wall, as if wounded or dead. "I think I got some of em", said Deuce. Suddenly, rounds were impacting the sand bags and cracking over their head. "Spartan 6, OP3...we have contact", muzzle flashes and zipping sounds sucked up the air around them. "Oh shit", they all hunkered down. Deuce intently returning fire, standing firm in position with the SAW's tripod neatly fitted between the shanty sand bagged fortifications. The radio erupted with calls from Spartan 6, Bronco 6 and Roughneck for a sit rep. The fire ceased momentarily. Smokey (AmTracs), Roughneck (CAAT), and White 4 (Tanks), all responded to the call and geared up to cordon off the area around the suspected "Ghost House". The silhouetted figures were gone, but the thermals still showed signs of a few heat signatures, looming between cracks in the wall, lying stationary on the deck. It also appeared that one of the suspected enemies had moved from that location, across the street, and was hiding behind the wall of an entranceway. The situation appeared to have scattered the cell, possibly wounding or killing at least two.

The OP Marines continually scanned with NVGs and their thermals, battery power dwindling. No one could see anything without some type of night vision from that distance in the dark. They feared it would be too late before the cordon could take place and the rest of them would get away. Spartan 6 gave the order to remain in place and wait for Spartan 3 (Charlie Third Platoon) to get there. Deuce was pumped up, yelling out updated sit reps every time he saw something. He was intently focused through the sights, finger straight, and off the trigger.

The kid had discipline. He wore a K-Bar on each side of his waist belt, volunteering to patrol down before Third platoon could get there. "I don't want someone else to have to clear because we engaged that house", but it was too late. Captain Quiet had already dispatched Third Herd to go do the dirt. It was an accountability and intelligence gathering issue. At that stage in the game, the battle was a wrap, but the brass needed to verify good intelligence, body counts, and BDAs (battle damage assessments). Since civilians were back in the city, the ROEs had changed drastically, and every fire engagement was to be highly scrutinized and investigated. Moke knew that. It was his head on the pike. He didn't feel good about it because he didn't want to risk the lives of his buddies to play CSI: Fallujah, but it wasn't his call.

An hour later, the cavalry arrived as the Third Herd QRF dismounted the AmTracs, CAAT and White 4 from the tanks followed in trace. It turned into quite an operation. It was nearly 3 am. Morning Prayer would soon echo from the minarets, and the sun would rise shortly thereafter. Moke manned the radio and walked them on target as they cleared each house along the way from bottom, up. The AmTracs threw grenades on the roof tops, and the tanks posted up, metabolizing JP8, with its familiar smell and jet propulsive emission. It was difficult to make out the location of the exact house on the map in respect to the view in the dark, but it was decided to be the second house on Block 824, bordering 804. Spartan 3 was bitching on the radio. It was a little personal. After burning down half the houses in the AO by stacking propane tanks and kerosene, he was a bit perturbed that his platoon was tasked with the mission. Third Herd was the biggest; the go to platoon for QRF missions. The sun was coming up, and a few birds chirped in the distance.

After clearing 5 or 6 houses in the general vicinity, the QRF Marines didn't find anything exclusive to indicate an enemy presence, accept a couple hundred bullet holes in the side of the wall of a rooftop courtyard. No bodies, no blood trails, no evidence of recent activity. Spartan 3 made haste over to OP3s position to get the full picture of what they allegedly said they saw. The lieutenant swaggered up to the sandbagged emplacement, as Moke pointed to his references and noted the, now sunlit, north facing wall that was eroded from a slew of 5.56 mm rounds. "Yeah, I know Corporal, I was just fuckin' over there.....You know you're a fuckin' asshole! What the fuck you think you're doing; having my guys come out here and clean up your shit"? "Well, sir...." "Shut the fuck up"....as the lieutenant turned his back and exited the rooftop back to the waiting AmTrac outside. He couldn't argue with an officer. Moke just swallowed it, smartly.

He followed Spartan 3 down the zigzagging staircase to board the AmTrac back to FB Pickering to debrief the command. When Moke opened the back hatch to the AmTrac, the entirety of the QRF detail stacked together inside, erupted with jeers and snarls at his expense. They busted his balls the whole way back to the FB. At the end of the day, fortunately, there was no incidence of fratricide with the ING and no one was killed or wounded in the botched debacle. Perhaps it was a lesson learned about making decisions, accountability, responsibility, and how no one wants it.

A few days later, Third Platoon went out on another clearing mission in the area of Block 824. They found a small cache and a few dead bodies, bandaged and bloody, two streets down from the "Ghost House". They discovered a long network of mouse holes in the side of the walls connecting through entire blocks of houses, living rooms, kitchens, and alleys, adding to the lore and elusiveness of the cat and mouse game. The Marines were still piecing together the modus operandi of the Fallujah insurgency. Two months after the invasion, clues offered no confirmation, just more questions.

January 10, 2005

Weed and Groucho managed to salvage a gas stove and a propane tank from one of the uninhabitable rooms on the third deck. They were hoping to concoct an improvised, gourmet creation from miscellaneous MREs that were rat fucked by somebody. They also managed to conjure up something suitable for expelling their excrement. They found an old, plastic water cooler, put a trash bag inside and sat on the rim of it. It served a practical function as a field expedient toilet. It worked pretty well for its purpose, but not much in the way of comfort. In the corner of the same room, there was a convenient hole for which to urinate in.

Their living quarters consisted of one room, a few rugs, and mattresses to sleep on. There were some plastic chairs and an old couch. The guys who manned the OP before them tried to make it homey. Weed found a radio and hooked up the antenna by splicing it to some wiring that ran to a satellite on the roof. Amazingly, it received good reception to the only English speaking radio station in Iraq, AFN (Armed Forces Network). It played a lot of classic rock and country music for their contemporary audience. It was cool to finally hear some news from around the world and get the college football highlights.

On one of the scavenging patrols around the perimeter, Groucho stumbled upon a little, white rabbit with his back to a corner, eyes wide open, and nibbling chips of paint off the wall. He was pretty fat, with a soft coat. He seemed pretty healthy, which was baffling to them. How was he in such great physical condition, not dehydrated and emaciated, like all the other domesticated cats and dogs wandering the streets? The flow of sustenance virtually came to a screeching halt a few months ago with the invasion. How did anything live there that had to forage for itself? It was odd, yet pleasant, and it offered the Marines a sense of luck. It seemed rational to try to explain away the significance of the rabbit, as if it was a fortuitous token. It was a male, with black spots over his eyes like a masked burglar. He was fed from the cucumbers and tomatoes brought by the ING for their nightly dinner. They named him George and he became their unofficial mascot. He brought some civility back into their lives; a calmness. It was kind of ironic to have a white rabbit masquerading around for the "Black Sheep". It's not always black and white; there are a million shades of gray.

Chapter 11
The Gas Station

January 15, 2005 - OP3 on PL Fran

Across the highway, to the northern side of Fran was one of two gas stations within Fallujah, but only one was still operating. The other one, near the Jolan District, was destroyed from American air sorties. A week had passed since several thousand civilians were allowed to return back into the city. The humanitarian aspect of the operation was well underway. Food was dispersed by the truckload, with a surplus of MREs and large plastic water bottles. There were very few cars driving around. Men, women, and children waited in a single line that stretched for miles down west Highway 10. The masses waited with gas canisters, plastic containers of all types, and some pushed their vehicles inch by inch as the line crept by the hour. Women and children were continuously being pushed further and further to the back as more men, cut into line in front of them.

The men always were more aggressive and yelled louder, getting their way. The women eventually succumbed as they languished with children in their arms. The owner of the gas station was thrilled for all the business, and liked to see the Marines walking around, ensuring order. Anything could happen. It was a fragile time. Someone could try to blow up the gas station. It was a legitimate target. Sabotaging it, ensured more chaos and would further the humanitarian crisis for the people living there. The Marines continued to patrol. Their presence was an indicator, and possibly a big target. It was just the four of them and a few ING. They were outnumbered, only equalized by their firepower. Fights and arguments broke out frequently in line from the frustrated people baking in the scorching sun. If a riot started, people would have to die because the Marines would have to fire into the crowds to disperse the mob of people just to protect themselves. What if that possibility had to happen, they thought?

They had training in crowd control, but not like this. After all, it was martial law, it was a temporary occupation. The Iraqis of OIF (Operation Iraqi Freedom), were subject to obeying all commands from the Marines or fear of being shot. Which was always likely, because all a Marine had to feel was an imminent threat of death, and he could return with deadly force, and it was easy to feel like everyone wanted to kill them, so it was easy to be ready to kill anyone they had to. The majority of the people were just desperate. They had fled with nothing and came back to nothing. They were gripping and clawing on survival and instinct, self-preservation. A Sudanese interpreter was among the crowd. He didn't carry a weapon, but was dressed in digital camouflage, with flak jacket and kevlar. He spoke Arabic, so naturally, people flocked around him to talk and overwhelm him with questions. He told the Marines in a heavy, African accent, "They say they hate Americans, because you've destroyed their homes, their city, and many are without food or a job".

The Marines replied it kind, "We hate them too. Those fuckin' pussies can't fight for their own homes? We fought for them and some died for it"! Marines are supposed to be impartial to the politics. There was too much rage and aggression to see through another lens. The Marine mentality would assume and even boast that if someone tried to take over their house back in the States and hold their family hostage, they would fight to the death to protect it with an arsenal of weaponry. Hell, that's the American way! That's how they beat the British in our own Revolutionary War....Why don't these civilians fight for their homes? That was the general assumption by the average grunt on the ground. Without delving too deep into the backdrop, Fallujah was unique because it enjoyed the privilege of being

Sunni, and the favor of the former Baathist Regime under Saddam. Sunni are also considered to be more conservative towards the interpretation of Islam. Many of the jihadists who answered the call to fight for the Holy Land were coincidentally Sunni, the more hardline, extremist types. With that said, the population of Fallujah is largely Sunni. By the very nature of the culture and ultimately by default, the people sympathized with the Sunni insurgency, aided and abetted them, fed them, sheltered them, and allowed their homes to be used as caches for weapons, despite suffering themselves by the atrocities performed by the insurgents, while enforcing Sharia Law.

Unfortunately, as in all wars, the civilians suffer the highest cost, but there was no love affair for the Marines, The Infidels. In the infantryman's mind, they say, "we give them food, reimburse them a check for damage to their homes, protect them, freed them from their insurgent captors, give them security, give them the gift of democracy....and they don't want it". In their minds, they just couldn't wrap their heads around that concept. It sounds like a pretty good deal for a bunch of inferior people who don't know any better, right? "They don't even know what freedom means", they say. Everyone is right and everyone is wrong. Everyone is getting fucked in some way. The Iraqis, the women and their kids, the Marines, even the insurgents. They were all pawned off into a war that was much bigger than a city of full of insurgents. The notion of democracy in the Islamic world is the quintessential oxymoron.

The Fallujans seem to have seen centuries of oppression. They wear it on their leathery faces. Women dressed in all black burqas signify that they are married women. Younger girls wear colorful garments and show their faces. The men adorn their typical full man dresses, with airy, fluffy white shirts, appearing just as comfortable as can be. However, it's interesting in contrast, that men always wear lighter shades of clothing, but married women are cloaked in a thick black cloth, a color that absorbs the most heat from the sun's radiation. From a Westerner's perspective, the Muslim World appears to be a very dark place, where people are prohibited from growing, evolving, or developing to their full potential. It's a barren, colorless landscape, intensely opaque to the eye. There is no grass, no vegetation, no apparent happiness, and also not remiss from the fact that their city just got leveled, but it goes much deeper than that.

The men just stare as the Marines walk by. It becomes a staring contest, tempering the desire to snatch his ass up in front of all of his friends, squatting on the corner, or just fuckin' blow all their heads off right there, in front of everyone. It would be so fuckin' easy!!! There was just a little smirk from the Marine as he looked down confidently, gesturing to his finger, tapping the trigger and clicking his weapon off safe. He passed an egregious "Salam" over his lips to ease the tension, never knowing if they were just awe-struck in their own daze and bewilderment, or if they were sizing up the Marines to kill them the next day. They remained constantly vigilant at the gas station. It always seemed something terrible was imminent. It was suspicious to see the same people, for one reason or another, walk by the VCP (Vehicle Check Point) back and forth, two or three times. Some of the teenagers would say "Hello mister". The kids waved with their other hand firmly gripping to their mother's side. People used the gas and kerosene to light the stoves in their house for cooking, run generators (because there was no electricity, no water services to the town), to light lanterns, and keep warm in the frigid January chill.

The issuing of identification cards, retinal scanning, gun powder residue testing, and metal detection apparatuses, all increased the efforts in efficiently processing people in and out of the city within the hours between a city-wide curfew. It required all civilians to be off the street and in their homes by 1800 (6pm). Cars were not allowed to be parked anywhere on the street at any time. Someone had left a white BMW in front of the gas station. Sabaa, the ING, called out to anyone who owned it several times, with no response from in the crowd. He asked once more before, slashing each of the tires with his knife. Just then, before slashing the last tire, a man came running from down the street. He had left his wife to get gas, while he attempted to get food at the Red Crescent. It sucked for him, but those were the rules.

That was what had to be done to enforce rules, or people abuse kindness for a weakness, gaining a mile with an inch. The reality of the situation had to be applied firmly to the people who were being subjugated. It was martial law...the Marines were the law. The mediocrity of the average Fallujan was overtly apparent, but there was no time for empathy or to contemplate their misfortune, whether it being a mistake or otherwise. The driver's side window was smashed in with the compensator of an M16 and searched. The man was forced to leave it in place, until they could be replaced in the morning because the tires were flat. The man couldn't have even rolled the car home if he had wanted to. Anyone loitering or milling around were suspect to arrest and/or possibly shot. Just before dusk, the streets which had been so lively and bustling during the day light hours receded into a ghost town within minutes. The mounted patrols and CAAT teams resumed absolute control. They stretched out their legs with the streets cleared. They owned the nights and by ways.

The mannerisms and customs of the Fallujans seemed routine. It was apparent from a first glance that it's a male dominated society and that women are second-class citizens in every facet of the culture. They carry the burden of the Islamic societal structure. From birth, women are taught to serve a man, and be worthy for marriage. And they are quickly bartered into an arrangement by the fathers of the two families, when, indeed, they are old enough to bear children. The dowry is a common tradition in the Islamic world. Women rarely have the opportunity to marry for love, or a man of their choosing. While searching and clearing houses for months, the Marines occasionally encountered personal effects, pictures, and jewelry that were left behind in the mass exodus. Pictures of newly wedded couples invoked eerie, nuances. The groom would always be smiling from ear to ear, showing off his prized trophy, and the bride, her face caked with makeup and bright, red lipstick, stoic with emotion, void of any indication that that day, that moment, was the happiest of her life.

In fact, under Sharia Law, it was the first day of her imprisonment and torture. From then on, she would always walk six paces behind her husband, carrying a basket of groceries on her head, with an infant child swaddled to her chest, and another toddler, lagging behind her feet as she struggled to keep pace with her husband's assertive stride. All the mosques have minarets, which ironically and characteristically, resemble that of a giant penis. Was this a blatant reminder of male domination and sexual oppression, an ode to the core values of a gender-segregated culture that exists in the Islamic World? The average grunts had no concept of what it implied. But it ultimately reflected a deep seated insecurity among Islamic men. The women cover themselves from their own identity, their own dignity as a human being. They keep women completely subordinate, and still practice the archaic, institution of polygamy. They engage in underworld taboos, like drinking black-market alcohol, fornicating with animals and homosexuals, and many are addicted to pornography. They live in a world of sexual oppression and rampant hypocrisy.

One day after completing a patrol around the area, the fire team stopped by the gas station to see the line unusually long. A lot of people had a sad story, trying to wheel and deal and hustle their way to the front of the line. The general rule at the gas station was one container was allowed to be filled per person. Two or more gas containers were not allowed. There wasn't enough gas per day to accommodate all the people in line, let alone to fill up multiple containers. There had to be some order and fairness. The Marines wouldn't allow chaos and anarchy to ensue. Sabaa walked down the line with a large knife, puncturing holes in the containers of people who carried two or more at a time. It was already late in the day, and the women were pleading with the Marines to allow them to get ahead of some of the men, because they had sick children, and desperately needed to cook and heat their homes.

The men were angry, because the women shouldn't have been talking to the Marines in the first place, exasperated by the fact that the women stood in their way of a profit. Without allowing the others to alternate for a chance to fill up, one of the men just strong armed the women aside. He was screaming obscenities as he continued filling and refilling the empty gas cans in the back of his truck to resell it down the street for a cheaper price. The women decried him, exposing his black market scam, as the Marines effectively removed the man at gunpoint and forced him to leave the scene without his truck. After witnessing the blatant disregard for the women in the line (many burdened with small children), Deuce threw his arms in the air, directing the people for their attention to be on him. "Ok people" he yelled in English, as Sabaa translated into Arabic, "we are going to have our first lesson in democracy. One line on this side for men, and one line on this side for women, each alternating at the gas pump...and if any of you women-beaters want to fight over it, you can meet the end of my muzzle".

It took a few seconds for Sabaa to catch up in translating to Arabic what Deuce had said. Immediately, the relieved, smiling faces of the women formed their own line, as the men erupted in blustering shouts and rants. The gas station was only going to be open for a few more hours, and hundreds of people had waited all day to get to their position in the line. There had to be a more efficient way, but this was it. There was only one working pump for thousands of needy gas containers in the city. When it closed for the day at 1630, people got really pissed off, the futile reality that their quest for the day was completely in vain. They would have to wait until the following day, starting at 0600 in the morning, when the gas station re-opened for business. They couldn't just camp out in line to save their spot, like kids waiting for tickets at a rock concert, because everyone had to be off the streets for the nightly curfew, otherwise, no one would have moved. Anything was better than gambling on another day without the basic necessities. The anxiety of an early morning spot in the gas line weighed heavy on their sleep. There were no trees to chop down or wood to burn. Their whole day had revolved around getting gas and kerosene to do the basic chores of daily living. Without it, life was stagnant.

With the sun cresting its head over the horizon, people were already lined up as soon as the curfew was lifted at 0600. A rumor had been circulating from the brief interludes between the grunts at the OPs and the mobilized CAAT patrols that frequented the AO. Tommy T was leaning off the side of his Humvee, munching on some stale crackers and cheese. "How the fuck do you guys sleep in there", asked Moke, alluding to the cramped, tiny compartment within the Humvee. "We don't", he replied, "we just kind of sit with our eyes closed and stretch a lot". The grunts thought they had it rough because they had to walk and hump their shit everywhere, but the CAAT guys were literally attached to four wheels, like some road warring tribe of the zombie apocalypse. Tommy had five fingers, but he only used "tree". His words were accompanied by a various degree of hand gestures. He usually offered up some sarcastic, Chicago-glazed, humor early in the morning, with an affinity for gangster movies, and the charisma of a back alley hustler. Known to frequent the watering holes of Waikiki, there was some history there.

The word was Battalion 1/3 was set to leave the city in the next week. "Get the fuck outta here man, are you serious? Don't be passing no bum scoop bro". Moke came down from standing post on the OP with a huge box. It must have weighed thirty pounds. It was filled with random candy and other accessories sent from the countless organizations, fundraisers, and church groups who funneled care packages to the troops from back in the States. After rat fucking what they wanted, they decided to give all the rest of it to the orphan kids, aimlessly trudging the streets in front of the gas station. "Mista, Mista...chocoleta. Mista, Mista...your watch...you give me? They eagerly crowded around him, circling and mobbing him like a school of piranhas. He just dropped the box on the ground after they clawed and pulled, tearing it apart, out of his hands. Candies exploded out of the box, everywhere, as a mass frenzy of kids, pushed and shoved, and fought for everything they could grab and stuff into their pockets. Some of the older males were lurking and tried to come in and push the kids out of the way, groping their greedy hands in the attempt to ransack some of the goods.

The Marines forcefully chased them away, but it only took a few minutes for the ground to be swept clean of every morsel they could muster. A lot of those kids were little, bad ass, gang stars. They lived on the street and ran in packs like hyenas. They spit on the ground everywhere and talked real fast. Especially the red heads, they were the worst. They would stab an unaware bystander swiftly with a sharp object and rob them blind if they could get away with it. They were hungry and desperate. There is nothing as dangerous as desperation, except martyrs, and Fallujah had them both.

At night, in a brief respite in the silence of the weary morning hours, there were some in- depth conversations via those little hand-held radios. Delirious and half-hallucinating on nicotine and caffeine, the watchman would click back and forth in between radio checks with the CP to toss around the meaning of life, about home and family. They talked about what they wanted to do, where they wanted to travel, religion, politics, sports, Hollywood gossip; Someone said Brittany Spears died! It passed the hours away, shivering in the cold, with a consistent breeze from the southeast, from the sea. Winds that blew for 300 miles on flat, empty desert before releasing from the air, little granules of sand that encrusted around the corners of their mouth. There is not much to say. A dry mouth needs water, some lubricant. "I should listen more to the guy at the other end, but I'm too busy talking about my dreams, my delusions, and my undiagnosed neurosis. I can't stop bouncing my foot to knee, foot to knee. This involuntary movement is driving me crazy", he thought. "I just need a full night's sleep, with no fuckin' interruptions, no fire watch, I tell ya. I just can't wait to get the fuck out of Iraq, you know what I mean................Hey bro, you there"?

Sometimes, it was better to just say nothing and listen. The traffic on the different radio frequencies made for some amusing entertainment. The verbiage, acronyms, and general repetition of radio communications were unique in their general protocol and descriptive chatter. "Smokey....this is Ramrod, interrogative, does Shitbrick know the deal with the whatchmacalit, question mark, over". The reply comes back shortly. "Ramrod....this is Smokey, negative, Shitbrick does not know the deal with the whatchumacalit, exclamation mark, how copy?, over". "Smokey....this is Ramrod, roger, that's a solid copy, Shitbrick does not know the deal with the whatchumalit...break...interrogative, should I tell him about the whatchumacalit, question mark, over". "Ramrod....this is Smokey, negative, period. Do not tell Shitbrick about Fiona and me, exclamation mark, period, over". "Smokey...this Ramrod, roger that, Shitbrick will not know anything, period, over and out".

The ING mission was a sham, but the Marines were ordered to work with them, to live with them, even trust their lives with them to a degree. Who's to say they wouldn't try to kill the Marines. Nothing could stop them if they decided to conspire. Although cautiously aware and vigilant, the Marines were not prepared for that possibility, and if so, nothing could stop the ING from inflicting a random act of green on blue fratricide. Deuce found a pistol in one of the house clearing missions. He had it strapped to his gear as a secondary weapon. He used it as a bartering chip and lost it in a game of poker with the ING. It turned into a big deal once they got their hands on it...playing with it, pointing it all over the place, and bragging about it to their peers. It wasn't a big deal, but it was a big deal. They all had weapons.

Anyone could shoot anyone, at any time. To the average guy on the ground, a pistol is like a token, a valuable souvenir. However, it was contraband, nonetheless, and smuggling or carrying unissued weaponry was a no go. One of the ING was a bit upset after the game. He started saying "Down with Bush...Bush no good". He kept repeating it with a murderous rage in his eye. He insisted on it again and again, as if he wanted to pick a fight with the Marines. Tensions ran high because a small quarrel could easily flare up into an international incident. These guys have been fighting, killing, and witnessing carnage for months. Everyone had a weapon. Anyone could blow anybody away, anytime. "What the fuck did you say motherfucker...you hear this guy. What the fuck, you trying to start some shit"? The Marines conferred amongst each other and their ING counterparts. The man, dressed in Iraqi, chocolate chip, desert fatigues, became even more emboldened and serious faced as his fellow soldiers chided him in Arabic. Something weird just set the guy off, and he wanted to convey is disloyalty to the Marines. Sabaa went to Moke and told him, "This man is no good...he is Alibaba", a term referring to "an insurgent". Seemed like some type of enemy infiltration, or just a madman.

Instead of lashing out, the disgruntled ING was eerily calm with contempt spewing from his eye balls. The Marines wasted no time. Desperately trying to subdue the urge to kill the Iraqi man where he stood, they made the call back to FB Pickering, explaining the increasingly volatile situation. It took all they could to muster the restraint to refrain from any type of bilateral incident which would most certainly headline the Marines, and become fodder for media outlets around the world. It's amazing to think of how potent the wrong action and/or decision can be and what it could mean to stability operations, and the overall mission.

The Marines, just mere 20 somethings, were put under insurmountable pressure and completely accountable for their decisions and professional standards of conduct at all times. It was part of the powerful and constantly looming, UCMJ (Uniform Code of Military Justice) There is no coincidence that the military has a separate justice system. However, the fact remained that it was just too easy to pull the trigger. That day could have resulted in a big, black eye for the American coalition effort and "Operation Iraqi Freedom". Instead, the Marine commanders immediately descended upon OP3 and assertively removed the disgruntled ING soldier. He was never seen again. The incident proved to be a newfound, measure of trust between the Marines and the ING. Especially with Sabaa, who had proven himself to be pretty reliable. After the "ING infiltrator" was removed, the tempo settled down and they resumed their normal working relationship.

Smoking from the hookah at night and drinking tea with the ING, seemed to reinforce that relationship. Days prior, on a patrol, Fathal, the young, complacent ING with the crooked smile almost shot off his own foot. They had bad habits in handling their weapons. He would always carry his AK-47 with one hand, pointing it down at the ground, flicking the safety on and off, while fingering the trigger at the same time. It was such blatant disregard for safety, but not because of any reckless abandonment. Fathal was just seriously ignorant, poorly trained, and completely aloof. "Pow"! A negligent discharge from his weapon sent a round right into the dirt, cratering a small hole just inches from his feet. He looked up in dismay.

Moke was standing right next to him, as granules of sand and rock sputtered off his face, his right ear muffled and ringing. "What the fuck are you doing", as Moke slapped him across his helmet, like a small boy being scolded from his father. Fathal just looked at him in embarrassment. What more could he do about it. Rip him a new asshole? Besides, that doesn't carry the same weight as if it were a US Marine. The ING were not abided by the same rules, the same enforcement of those rules. It kind of just gets overlooked in the hope that it doesn't happen again. That is a foreign concept in a grunt's mind. Normally, he would have been instantly remediated, chided, and over all, fist fucked by the very system that he was obliged to. From the regimented, highly trained, and well-disciplined perspective of the Marine Infantryman, everything about the ING soldier was baffling and just considered overall, nasty. What could they do?

Well, there was one thing they could do. Moke knew just the trick to teach Fathal a lesson he would soon never forget. He had a tube of Bengay in his patrol pack. He approached Fathal with it, sort of mimicking circular rotations around his genital area. Moke proceeded to entice Fathal with rewarding groans and sounds of pleasure. He motioned to him, prompting him to try it. Fathal looked eagerly with his crooked smile and jutting, front teeth. He took the Bengay, squeezed out a generous amount in his hand, and reached down into his pants, slathering it all over his crotch. At first it felt cool and refreshing on his testicles, exhibiting a comforting facial expression. Seconds later, he began to sweat profusely, as his face turned red and disconcerting. He started running around in circles screaming, "my dick on fire....Owwwwwww"!! He spent the rest of the night wiping down his genitals with baby wipes and positioning his crouch in front of a small fan. They all laughed and cackled incessantly, and even Sabaa made fun of him for being so naive. "That'll teach you to finger-fuck your trigger well again".

The Grenade Incident

It's interesting how things can turn full circle in the most unexpected ways. No one was completely immune to the occasional error. Working and handling an array of explosives and munitions is a perpetual affair. After a while, complacency or just simple mistakes can cost a person their own life. In combat, it always gets to a certain point where one realizes they could be potentially more dangerous to themselves than the enemy could. This often occurs during the consistent handling, use, and sometimes abuse, of a seemingly limitless supply of ammo and grenades.

Country was doing his usual resupply rounds for the day to all the OPs via the trusted workhorse of the grunts, the AmTracs. He would coordinate the link up via radio with the details and the Marines would meet in front of the OPs to carry away cases of water, MREs, 5.56 ball and link ammunition, and 40 mm grenades and M67 frags. Sometimes, he even came driving up actually driving the damn AmTrac. He'd be all decked out with the crew chief's helmet on. Some things just always looked funny and out of place. And the vision of Country driving an AmTrac was one of them. He had already ran through resupplying the OPs and radioed to OP3 that he was stopping by again to give some tangible, pertinent intelligence that he needed to pass on. Weed and Groucho were transitioning the guard watch and Cowboy was sleeping, so Moke got up to answer the radio call.

"Spartan 1 to OP3, I'll be over there in about 2 mikes", Country dialed over the radio. "Roger that, solid copy", Moke confirmed, as he set down the radio, and quickly started donning his heavy flak and kevlar helmet. Anytime they went outside, full gear and weapon was required. The sun was going down, the sky turning the same pinkish, reddish- orange that accompanied the closing of another day. Weed had strategically placed booby traps with some trip wire grenades and flares around the perimeter, at the base of the building that housed OP3. It was almost 1800 hours, some 45 minutes later, since the first time that Country came by the OP on the resupply mission for the night. Weed had checked and reset the traps on the perimeter after Country rattled away in the AmTrac the last time. The last booby trap that he always fixed in place was a trip wire attached to a grenade with the pin pulled and the spoon held down with just enough pressure from a piece of concrete, to hold it in place. He carefully and neatly, fashioned the wire along the first set of steps in front of the gate. The gate was effectively secured along with a huge, heavy piece of steel that they slid in front of it for extra protection which was, ultimately, the only entrance to the building. Everyone at the OP was fully aware of the booby traps and their locations.

Moke, laden with his gear and weapon, ran the six flights of steps, zigzagging down the stairway. He came to the bottom, slinging his weapon to grab a hold of the imposing piece of metal barricading the gate, as he slowly slid it open. He removed the steel rod wedged in the gate and forced it open. Took a step outside, and then down a step, and another. In the temporary distraction of Country revisiting the OP, the monotony of the security posture, and just sheer complacency, Moke took the last step before reaching the dusty, graveled surface. In doing so, he felt a slight tug at the tip of his boot. In the dimly lit dusk of the day, he could see the subtle glisten of the fishing wire, as his eyes followed it up and to his right. Almost simultaneously, the grenade was jarred from underneath the rubble of concrete and rolled a few rotations, stopping next to his right foot. Within a few nanoseconds, his brain processed the magnitude of the situation.

The world evolved into slow motion, emitting pulsating shockwaves throughout his body, where every acutely defined detail was instantly preserved in a wrinkle. The snap of a finger, fortunately, becomes an eternity in time. He just kept thinking, ok, foot...grenade...foot...grenade. "Wow, what a beautiful moment, I wish it would last forever. Am I dreaming? Am I really this fucked? Am I really that fucking retarded to trip my own fuckin' grenade"?! "Ahhhhhhh !!!!", he exclaimed out loud, in silence, because he couldn't muster even the girliest screech. Within all that was transpiring in those brief, but poignant moments, he didn't have a flash of his life, he didn't pray to a god...he just ran faster than he'd ever run before. With a humble stroke of luck and a little grace, a concrete support pillar was steps away. It was conveniently enough to encompass the width of his shoulders, four ways around, vetting his refuge. With each quick step towards the pillar, he worried he might trip and fall, thus succumbing to the torrent of hot shrapnel fragments up his ass and spine.

Just as he got in front of the pillar, he made himself as small as he could, hugging his back towards the concrete slab, arms straight at his side. "One-one thou..." "Boom"!! The concussion rocked the beam he was leaning against. Shards of rubble blew out past him, shielded by the pillar, like a bubble. The whoosh of debris and not a single bit of anything struck his body and extremities. He was in shock. He was elated to be unscathed. But immediately felt like the biggest dumbass in Fallujah. He was inundated with a slew of emotion, compacted with the adrenaline, filled moments of narrowly escaping death. All he could think of was the Marines that would show up at his parent's house in full, Dress Blue uniform. "On behalf of a grateful nation, we regret to inform you that your son was killed in Iraq because HE WAS FUCKIN' STUPID"!!!! That would have been his legacy, especially considering the irony of it all. The same guy who berated and hounded his men to be squared away at all times, pay attention to detail, be vigilant, don't get complacent, etc, "got himself killed with his own grenade". It would be so tragically absurd, that it would actually turn into a funny joke after the unfortunate reality of his death wore off. A Marine can't die like that and hope that people would feel anything for him other than sheer pity. That story would have been told and gossiped at funerals, football games, and bars for years to come. It just doesn't get more real than that.

The dust and smoke blew right up through the bowels of the building, funneled up through the zigzagging stairway. All the guys peered out over the balcony from the top level waiting to see if Moke was lying dead at the bottom. Slowly, gradually, the black smoke dissipated. Moke was standing there, looking up with an embarrassing smile. "It's ok, I didn't get hit by anything", he said humbly. "You dumb fuck...that was really fuckin' dumb, you know how fuckin' lucky you are"? , they all jeered him. He just sat down and let it soak in, thinking he was too "short" for that shit. He was going to get out of the Marines in a few months. It was almost the end of January, and he was slated to be out by the end of March. A minute later, Country arrived to see the huge plume of smoke. "What happened"? "I tripped my own grenade coming back down", Moke explained. "You dumb fuck...you know how fuckin' lucky you are"? , he bellowed. "Yeah, they told me already".

Chapter 12
Korean Village

January 21, 2005 - Exiting Fallujah

After seventy five days of continuous urban combat operations for the Second Battle of Fallujah, the Lava Dawgs of Battalion 1/3 were relieved in place at FB Pickering by Battalion 3/4 and pulled out of the city. All fire teams, squads, and special detachments returned to their respective platoons and companies. From there, the five companies of Battalion 1/3, to include Alpha, Bravo, Charlie, Weapons, and H&S Companies returned briefly to Camp Fallujah about 4 miles to the North of the actual city limits. Upon arrival, the Marines were given the opportunity for a long, hot shower, chow hall food (which is like a buffet), PX runs, and some hard won "down time". There was a good, 72 hour break for the Marines, under the general safety of the largely, fortified and guarded encampment. There was no wind for the cold, but instead, it rained every day, slow and fat, turning the dusty sand to mud puddles. It didn't matter much to the Marines because they were finally given the promised and long-awaited, Christmas ration of two beers per man. It became a bit of a frat party.

A bunch of dudes hugging and loving on each other, singing songs, with some jolly, good banter. Some of the Marines quietly busted out some contraband bourbon from out of nowhere, and were catching a nice buzz after so many months without a single drop of alcohol. Talking about girls and probing porn magazines, making a beeline for the porta-shitters with a personal roll of toilet paper. They were mostly all completely celibate for the entire deployment. Some guy, somewhere in the battalion, probably made it happen with a Wook (female Marine) or an Army mattress in Kuwait, but that's a higher echelon possibility, maybe.

It wasn't like Vietnam when Marines could mosey into a ramshackle brothel with three dollars or try to persuade a local. This was Muslim-land. Except for the flood of civilians back in the city a few weeks from their departure, there wasn't even the happenstance of ever seeing a woman in the flesh, let alone seeing her face, close up. Usually, only young girls, like teenagers didn't cover their faces with clothe, and only pedophile types were eroticized by that. After remaining sexless for 9 months, being flaccid was inconsequential. The Marines were just in awe and elated to be alive, having a beer with the guys who remained through the thick of it all and toasting to those that didn't. It was a special moment, a conviction of brotherhood and camaraderie.

The party was short lived when the battalion was assigned orders to deploy into several key areas in the Anbar Province to secure the first "free" Iraqi elections slated to happen on January 31, 2005, throughout the entire country. Charlie Company, specifically designated as the helicopter company for the 31st MEU, was ordered to gear up with all that they carried and were flown via CH-53D Sea Stallion helicopters out to Al-Asad Airbase in the northern part of Iraq. Al-Asad was a sprawling complex, formerly an Iraqi Air Force base for Saddam's military. It already had an established airstrip and hangar facilities, so naturally, the US military just built upon that after occupying it, but several of the former buildings remained. For the Marines, the base served as a transition point. They were afforded tents in a designated area with their own chow hall, etc., out away from the rest. It was always best to separate Marines from the other services whenever possible. However, there was also a rickety shuttle that would drive the Marines around the huge base to go to the PX, other chow halls (plural) and leisure facilities. Those instances always reminded the grunts that, experiences in a combat tour vary to several different degrees.

January 26, 2005

Charlie Company received its orders to chopper down to Camp Korean Village, on the outskirts of a town called Rutbah. It was the last major town before the main highway split off into two directions, one way heading to the border of Jordan and the other to the border of Syria, through the vast expanse of the western Iraqi desert. From there, the company would split up into platoons and squads and deploy out from there and integrate with other units to fill the demanded security plans. The camp was called Korean Village because, ironically, it was an actual town constructed for North Korean nuclear physicists who lived there when working on the development of Saddam Hussein's alleged nuclear weapons program. Summarily, under the pretense of the stockpiling of "weapons of mass destruction", Iraq was invaded by the US in the early spring of 2003. Accordingly, no evidence was ever produced to support those allegations.

The platoons were assigned to "sticks" for their flight via helicopters to Korean Village. The two sticks were typically made up of 24 Marines, which was considered full capacity for the CH-53D helicopter. The crew members were from a Heavy Marine Helicopter Squadron 361 based in California, and attached to the 31st MEU. It was a heavy, large propeller, Vietnam era, helicopter, used as the typical workhorse machine in support of Marine operations by flying them and their supplies back and forth. That day, they were all up early staging their gear together, preparing for the flight. It was a "hurry up and wait" kind of thing. Two sticks made up the load of one helicopter and they always flew in pairs, so up to 50 Marines could be moved at a time. Charlie Company was made up of roughly 150 men, so there would be at least three separate flight evolutions for the day to Rutbah to get all of them there. First Platoon was the smallest, so they were all together on one stick and made the flight late in the morning. It took about an hour to touch down at Camp KV.

Staring out the back of the helo, there was an endless barren landscape of nothingness. Occasionally, there would be a speck of human existence as a shanty, Bedouin dwelling and some camels came into view from above. Otherwise, it looked like the surface of a faraway moon...nothing appeared habitable. Eventually, as they flew further to the West, the flat sands turned to rocky outcrops and plateaus. Shortly, jutting up a few hundred feet and then flatly surfaced. Minutes later, the first stick touched down on a small helicopter flight line at Camp KV. As the ramp lowered, the Marines shuffled off the "bird" toting all their gear. The second helicopter promptly landed behind the lead. The rotors swooshing and the smell of aviation fuel as the crew chiefs wave signals to the pilots.

The Marines were ushered along to another group of tents, where they would stow their gear and get accommodated for their short tenure. They got the scoop of the area, the basic amenities, and the location of what and where, etc. It wasn't anything impressive, just another US military outpost in the middle of the desert. Korean Village, itself, was in the back of the small base. It looked like a small cul de sac, neighborhood made up of concrete houses, now occupied according to the pecking order of the camp elite. Just a little before the evening meal had started in the hastily, constructed chow hall, the second wave of two sticks landed with a mix of guys from other platoons, mostly Third and Weapons Platoon guys. The day was drawing to a close and the sun set on CKV. It was cold and the wind was blowing hard that day. The Marines stayed in their tents mostly to avoid the pelting sand that was carried in the wind. As it was already dark, it was expected that the remaining Marines would fly out the next day. The Marines at CKV settled in for the night in their racks, bundled in their poncho liners.

Meanwhile, back at Al Asad Airbase, the last two remaining sticks were loading up to take off. It was well past midnight. They were heavily loaded with a few extra men. They had to spread load some of them apart on the two birds because they each had over the maximum capacity of 24 heads per stick. In effect they were loaded to up to 27 per stick for the last flight to CKV, including, the four flight crew. At the last minute, Marines were switched and shuffled back and forth between the two helicopters on the flight line. The stick leaders counting and verifying the manifest list with the crew chiefs. The powerful, whipping blades of the rotors added to the commotion and the confusion in communication. After each stick was finally crammed in, the birds slowly lifted into the cold and windy desert, night sky.

The weather was bad, with torrential, wind storms blowing out in the open desert of western Iraq. Flying at night, the helicopter pilots were used to wearing NVGs to see, however it did them no good to increase their visibility. About forty-five minutes into the turbulent flight, there was an abrupt flash and apparent explosion on the ground. The Marines on the other helicopter had a very limited view and many had no clue of what had just happened. The helicopter started moving erratically up and down. The crew chief in the front of the bird was erratically moving very fast and sticking his head out of the window, looking down. It was obvious that something was wrong, but it was so loud inside the cabin, no one could hear each other speak, even yelling as loud as they could. The next five minutes seemed like an eternity as the CH-53 hovered onto the deck of the flight line at Camp Korean Village. The crew chief was irately yelling at the Marines to get off the aircraft immediately. When they exited the bird, they ran off the tarmac with their gear, but there was no second helo in trace. It wasn't clear what had happened, but the flight crew was expressing extreme duress for some reason. After quickly pushing the Marines off, the remaining helicopter took off again and flew out of sight. Moments later, the Marines were briefed by their Staff Sergeant, that the other helicopter had crashed, and a rescue party was being assembled to the scene. It was a feeling of utter dismay, shock, grief, guilt, and disbelief. There were more questions than anyone had answers to.

According to official reports from the US government, at approximately 1:20 am, the pilot of the CH-53D Sea Stallion Helicopter became disoriented in the inclement sandstorm, possibly suffered temporary vertigo, and flew the aircraft straight into the ground. There were no survivors. Twenty-six Marines and one Navy Corpsman were killed, including the four flight crew members onboard. Immediately upon arriving at the scene of the crash, some 15 miles from Camp Korean Village, the first responders rushing out in their Humvees were held back and ordered to stand down with the rescue. The Marines aboard the helicopter were laden with ammunition, grenades, rockets, and the contents of that were cooking off and exploding from the fiery blaze.

Rockets were flaring out into the sky and intensely heated machine gun rounds, popped off and went zipping in every direction. The crash site was cordoned off, and the responders were forced to wait until the fire and explosions subsided before assessing any possible survivors and damage. Based on the firsthand witness account to the scene, it was presumed that no one was alive. The next day, when the sun arose, the crash site revealed an impact crater several feet deep. It was charred and littered with remains and twisted pieces of metallic debris. To the repute of the Marines, an affiliated Al-Qaeda group claimed responsibility for the downed aircraft, citing they shot it down with a surface to air missile. According to official US reports, it was deemed to be false after investigations concluded that the reason for the crash was based on pilot error.

They had just survived three months of intense combat operations and were within two weeks of leaving Iraq to begin heading back home and to their families. Some of the crash victims had children that were born during their deployment that they never had a chance to see. With six other military personnel killed in an ambush and IED attacks across the country, that day remained the single, deadliest day of combat operations during the Iraq War for US troops.

It was a tragic, gut wrenching loss for the Marines of BLT 1/3. It would not be clear until the names were read allowed the following day, who the crash victims were. No one was allowed any type of communication to people back home, until the military could officially notify the families of the deceased. That 72 hour period was the hardest for everyone, with agony and anguish to an inexhaustible degree for the families and Marines alike.

Killed January 26, 2005:

Charlie Company, First Battalion, Third Marines

Staff Sgt. Brian D. Bland, 26, Weston, Wyoming
Lance Cpl. Jonathan E. Etterling, 22, Wheelersburg, Ohio
Sgt. Michael W. Finke, 28, Huron, Ohio
1st. Lt. Travis J. Fuller, 26, Granville, Massachusetts
Cpl. Timothy M. Gibson, 23, Hillsborough, New Hampshire
Cpl. Richard A. Gilbert, 26, Montgomery, Ohio
Cpl. Kyle J. Grimes, 21, Northampton, Pennsylvania
Lance Cpl. Brian C. Hopper, 21, Wynne, Arkansas
Petty Officer 3rd Class John D. House, 28, Ventura, California
Lance Cpl. Saeed Jafarkhani-Torshizi, 24, Ft. Worth, Texas
Cpl. Steven P. Johnson, 24, Covina, California
Cpl. Sean P. Kelly, 23, Gloucester, New Jersey
Lance Cpl. Allen Klein, 34, Clinton Township, Michigan
Cpl. Timothy A. Knight, 22, Brooklyn, Ohio

Lance Cpl. Fred L. Maciel, 20, Spring, Texas
Cpl. James L. Moore, 24, Roseburg, Oregon
Cpl. Nathaniel K. Moore, 22, Champaign, Illinois
Lance Cpl. Mourad Ragimov, 20, San Diego, California
Lance Cpl. Rhonald D. Rairdan,20, San Antonio, Texas
Lance Cpl. Hector Ramos, 20, Aurora, Illinois
Lance Cpl. Gael Saintvil, 24, Orange, Florida
Cpl. Nathan A. Schubert, 22, Cherokee, Iowa
Lance Cpl. Darrel J. Schumann, 25, Hampton, Virginia
1st Lt. Dustin M. Shumney, 30, Vallejo, California
Cpl. Matthew R. Smith, 24, West Valley, Utah
Lance Cpl. Joseph B. Spence, 24, Scotts Valley, California
Lance Cpl. Michael L. Starr, 21, Baltimore, Maryland

HMH-361

Capt. Paul C. Alaniz, 32, Corpus Christi, Texas
Capt. Lyle L. Gordon, 30, Midlothian, Texas
Lance Cpl. Tony L. Hernandez, 22, Canyon Lake, Texas
Staff Sgt. Dexter S. Kimble, 30, Houston Texas

Jan 28, 2005 - En route from Rutbah

Despite how absurd, tasteless, and seemingly inappropriate it might be, the mission still had priority. It still had to be executed and accomplished. The mission to secure the first free elections in Iraq was inevitable. In fact, it was entirely appropriate that the Marines grieve shortly, and return to their duties. That's what Marines do, they execute orders in the face of adversity and adapt to, seemingly, impossible situations.

The platoons from Charlie Company were given their orders to disperse to various outposts in the farthest western regions of the Anbar Province. Most of Second Platoon was killed in the crash, except for six members. Third Platoon deployed to a nearby town called Hit, where they were to conduct security patrols around the polling sites. First Platoon was divided up in the two squads, Fish's squad went out to Waleed, a border town near Syria, and Moke's squad went to Trebil, a border town near Jordan. They were tasked with the same objective as the others, but essentially operating and asserting orders from within the integrity of the squad. It was new and refreshing to have complete operational independence, without all the scrutiny and micromanaging from the company headquarters.

They caught a ride with the weekly patrol and resupply from a convoy of Humvees that routinely made the trip out to the FOB (Forward Operating Base) at Trebil, a lonely Marine outpost 500 meters from the border of Jordan. The Motor

Transport guys proceeded to give them a brief and a rehearsal on convoy operations. They tried hard to assert their "extensive combat experience" while driving the single lane highway to Trebil, which were virtually null with IEDS. "Now!", the Gunny evoked, "what are the immediate action responses if we encounter an IED along the way"? Most of the grunts in the squad just kind of smiled and shook their head. "Look, Gunny, with all due respect, we just came from "the shit", we really don't need to be quizzed on immediate action", Moke interjected. "Well..., he stuttered, uhhhh, ok, but you know we drive this route frequently, so we can't get complacent". "Roger that, we'll pull our weight"! When they acquisitioned their Humvees for the transit, some random Motor T, Marine was standing in the turret behind a 240G medium, machine gun. "Wait, who are you"? , asked Moked. "I'm Wells, the mechanic". "Mechanic"?! , Moke exclaimed. "Oh Hell No...No....No...We keep unit integrity over here, so you're gonna have to go somewhere else. We'll man our own gun, bro". The POG (Personnel Other than Grunt) mechanic just kind of looked down and climbed out of the turret, quietly going to the Gunny to be reassigned to a different truck.

The Motor T guys started whispering amongst each other. "Man, just let em' do what they want, they seem like some salty-ass, ornery, fuckers". It was pretty ridiculous how POGs always wanted to try to assert their combat prowess. "Every Marine is a rifleman", gets drilled into their head so much, they actually believe it. "Do you even gun, bro"? It was easy to notice the guys who haven't seen much combat because they were so energized and eager to get shot at.

The convoy left Camp Korean Village for the nearly 100 mile trek west to Trebil. The long, desolate highway bared resemblance to the infamous Route 66 in the Southwestern US, meandering through desert nothingness on both sides, but remarkably paved and in good condition. Manning the 240G machine gun in the turret at 65 mph carried the same exhilaration of a Harley ride, the intoxicating beauty, and inextricable solitude of the infinite, vastness of the desert. The scene was reminiscent of a clip from the highly acclaimed movie, "Mad Max: Beyond the Thunder Dome. The FOB at Trebil was literally, a dead end. A small, circular encampment, near a border inspection station, in which eighteen wheeled semi-trucks and trailers parked up, bumper to bumper, like a traffic jam, for several miles. None of them moved. The drivers rested under the shade that the massive trailers provided. Sometimes, they would have to wait days and sleep underneath their trucks to make passage over the border.

Frequently, shady business deals and activity occurred because of the close proximity to the Jordanian Border, in which fighters, weapons, and supplies were constantly being smuggled into Iraq to support the extremist war effort. The FOB was occupied by Marines from an Artillery Battery out of Lejeune, Sierra 5/10, and some reservist grunts from 1/23. The Artie guys were slated as regular grunt, trigger pullers, because they had no artillery pieces at the FOB, except a mortar pit. In their four months manning the outpost, they claimed to have only been attacked a few times, once from a VBIED (Vehicle Borne, Improvised Explosive Device) that they rammed through the gate, which killed two Marines, and a few sporadic firefights, but nothing extensive besides that. It seemed like a relatively easy going place, little to know action, but that was dangerous. That always bred a comfortable, complacency. It always seemed like they were being watched, and they were. A hundred pair of eyes befell them each day, making notes of their movements, patrol routes, manpower, equipment, tactical demeanor, etc. The chow hall was a few levels below mediocre. The chow was served A-rats, basically, heated canned food. It was also the next best thing to the dreaded and over allocated, MRE (Meal Ready to Eat).

During those six days in Trebil, the squad conducted several mounted and dismounted patrols throughout the area. They also assisted the other units, by sharing the load of manning the posts around the FOB. Not much happened in the way of action. They snatched up a few suspicious vehicles at night, but produced little to no results. Their presence was enough to thwart any planned attack in the border town during the ensuing, electoral process. On January 31, 2005, the first, Free Elections to vote for a new president and other government positions in Iraq commenced. In Trebil a shallow trickle of voters braved their way to the polling station, but yielded very few ballots. In Hit, 10 miles outside of Rutbah, where Third Platoon was providing security, not one, single person showed to cast a vote. Their efforts within their AO to secure and encourage the electoral process mostly proved to be in vain. The insurgency lay in the shadows, deeply embedded, and tallied those who would be courageous enough to vote; threatening to kill them and their families.

To the Marines, the lack of accountability the Iraqis showed for their own lives and future was unfathomable. The right to vote is a big deal. Many of them died, including civilians to ensure that possibility. The Charlie Corps Marines had just lost twenty-nine of their brothers employing that effort. They empathized with civilians for the fear and repercussion associated with a vote, but it was their country, their opportunity to galvanize as one nation. A nation that has long been fraught with secular and ethnic divides. However, in the country as a whole, some seventy-two percent of all registered voters cast a ballot, largely from Shiite populated areas, including Baghdad. Many of the Sunni minority in Anbar Province feared their abdication from power would invite harsh reparations from years of Sunni rule under Saddam Hussein.

On February 2, the squad conducted its last combat patrol of the deployment. They had, by some miracle, completed their last mission with "all hands" remaining. They moved along the patrol route vigilant, but with a salty, swagger. The Marines stepped assertively, flowing like a choreographed ballet, executed hundreds of times before. Despite their inexperience prior to deploying to a combat zone, they had proven their effectiveness as a cohesive, fighting unit. The town was quiet. Their war was over.

The next day, after an early breakfast, the squad packed up and exited the wire of the FOB. In a patrol formation, they spread out in two sticks in an open swath of desert for the extraction back to Al Asad via CH-46 Sea Knights, the smaller twin propeller, Marine counterpart to the CH-53. They could hear the distinctive sputter of the twin rotors, miles off in the distance. Faintly the two gray specks appeared, like flies, lofting closer, and then hovering smoothly to the deck. The familiar onslaught of dust and sand encompassed every crevice on their bodies, but no man uttered a complaint as they vigorously, loaded up for the ride back. The thought of flying in a helicopter again after the crash just a week before, was a brief interlude in their minds, overshadowed by the final, unbelievable thought of "mission complete".

February 8, 2005 - Leaving Iraq

After the entire company was pulled off the lines and made whole again, it was a glorious revival of audacity and hope. It was like Christmas. They gorged themselves in the chow hall three times a day. They took advantage of every luxury and modern convenience. They took showers every day. Adjusting back to some relative comfort felt good. It was a kind of elation that couldn't be expressed with words. There was at least some temporary solace in the thought of being so close to home. Whatever "home" meant. Some of the more senior Marines who had carried leadership billets during the deployment were at the end of their contracts with the government. They willfully and happily, relinquished command of their responsibilities. The integrity of the original squads were broken down and restructured as new leaders and a new agenda commenced. The endless toil of gear accountability, inventory lists, turn-in, and contraband inspections, for unauthorized war trophies like weapons, grenades, and knives, etc. repeated itself. The Marines were thoroughly stripped of all ammunition and explosives prior to leaving the country.

Finally, after a few days of all that madness, they carried their shit and crammed into a C-130. Straddled nut to butt, they took off from Al-Asad Airbase with vomit inducing, evasive maneuvers to avoid potential rocket or surface to air, missile attempts at the aircraft. The G-force of the steep inclined takeoff pressed them together, succumbing to the pressure, they endured it. Then down on a hard flexing, roll to the right and back up again. It was loud inside the cargo plane. The piercing sounds of mechanical propulsion fighting back at the Earth's gravitational forces. Some Marines took their helmet off, cupping it near their mouth in the event of full abdominal release. About 45 minutes later, as the Marines drifted off into a deep slumber, pressed firmly against one another, they were jolted awake by a stiff and abrupt landing. As the C-130 pulled back on the brakes and slowed to a smooth taxi, shouts emanated from within the plane's cabin. "Welcome back to Kuwait"!!! Hoots and cheers quickly followed with clapping hands. It was officially over. They were in the "safe, friendly confines of their ally", which had been liberated fourteen years earlier by US forces in the Persian Gulf War of 1991.

Immediately upon arriving in Kuwait, the company took away their weapons and stored them in a large shipping container. It was further assurance that the mission was really over for them. They had toted their weapons around for more than eight months, and now felt somewhat naked without them slung to their sides. In the days that followed, they got used to the accommodations at Camp Virginia. They held a memorial service for the 50 Marines from Battalion 1/3 that had given their lives during the deployment. It was the highest loss of life suffered among all the participating infantry battalions of the operation, including the helicopter crash which remained the single deadliest day of the Iraq War. They erected fifty, separate memorials, known as a "Battlefield Cross", on display out in the Kuwaiti desert. Fifty Marines held the dog tags of their fallen comrades in their hands. As the Marine's name was read aloud in formation, the bearer would step forward and adorn the memorial with the fallen Marine's identifying set. It was a solemn reminder of the hard fought sacrifice of so many brave Marines.

Many of the short timers were slated to fly out to Okinawa en route to Hawaii, separate from the others who would re-embark back on the USS Essex. The ship was scheduled to make a Port Call in Pattaya Beach, Thailand. Even the thought of that wasn't enough to get some of the Marines to extend a month or two. "Shit man, you know how much fucked up shit can happen in a month? I'm cutting my losses, lest I get NJP'd (Non-Judicial Punishment)on the homestretch and put on an administrative hold. Nope, I did my time, my contract is up. Peace Out"! That was the general consensus among the shortest of the short timers. Better to get out, than get fucked by the green weeny anymore. Redeployment back to the States is another animal entirely. That's when problems occur with "decompression", including alcohol, drugs, DUI, fights, and general mischief. When retained as sole property of the US government for four years and then seduced with the prospect of bonuses and re-enlistment contracts, the smart money says "cash out and get out". "Once a Marine, always a Marine. So why re-enlist"?

Chapter 13
E.A.S. – End of Active Service

So there I was...four years and three deployments later. I was salty, but brand new. We landed back in Okinawa on March 5, 2005. Camp Hansen was just a terrible, recurring dream. I spent more time on that island than any other, going in and out, and back again. They always had strict rules about Liberty in Okinawa, so it was more of a general confinement to military bases only. They had an E-Club and served Mongolian BBQ twice a week. Those were a few of the perks. Since WWII, Marines had literally raped and pillaged that tiny Pacific island for decades and by now they were fuckin' sick of us. We couldn't drive (unless you were an officer, of course), taxis were a rip off, and there were constant drunken brawls and the threat of arrest looming at every dungy, little joint there was at Gate 2 Street. However, I discovered a modestly, quaint sushi bar that was only open during daylight hours in Kinville. It was the only place on that whole damn rock that I ever found draft beer with an ice, cold mug. It was brilliant, an added slice of comfort. Ahhh, it was just nice relishing those brief moments of solitude, being alone, but far from lonely.

It took me three years and more than a dozen attempts to actually find the place, but when I did, I heard a harmonious, chorus singing in my head. I never had time to really enjoy the fascinating beauty and culture of the Okinawan people. I had spent many a day wasting in the barracks at Hansen. The Command always put down so many restrictions to Liberty to inevitably deter Marines from venturing outside the confines of the base, or face severe retribution if caught doing something stupid in town. A lot of guys just saved money and sat around playing 8v8, marathon tournaments of HALO on XBox.

But this time, I would only be there for about 10 days. I had walked the modern city streets of Naha and the narrow village roads of Kin. I had seen the "Banana Show" and fornicated with a few old, whores. I had visited Hacksaw Ridge and Sugar Loaf Hill, the sight of bloodily, contested battles against the Japanese. I walked through the tunnels and heard the echoes of suffering and brutality. And there was much beauty to the limestone parapets that jutted the countryside. However, this was the last time I would ever see it again.

The very last order of business I had in Okinawa was to turn in my CIF gear (Central Issue Facility). For an Infantry Marine, this is a big deal. All the gear that you have toted around for years, some extremely valuable, others just arbitrary pieces of equipment that you were responsible for paying back to the government if it was lost. Some guys could accrue several thousand dollars in debt for lost items. But fortunately, coming back from a combat zone offered some leniency. Because of the nature of the experience, most items were simply considered "a combat loss". Congruently, for a grunt, not having gear meant not having to train. Not having to train meant that you didn't have shit else to do but jerk off and play HALO. Aside from the actual day that you are separated from the military, turning in CIF gear was the culminating event to EASing. It was like, literally and figuratively, a weight was lifted from your shoulders.

The days were numbered, howling the old adage, "you can't stop time". Freedom is within sight. There was the light at the end of the tunnel. And I had no plan. I was so enthralled with being liberated, that I detested structure, routine, and having a plan. The first lesson I learned as an infantryman was Plan A usually goes to shit in the first 10 seconds, so have a Plan B and even Plan C. In my stubborn rational, I thought. "That's why people have heart attacks at the age of 50. That's why people retire and then die, having never spent their money. That's what successful people do. I didn't give a shit about that". I was alive. I wanted to live my own way. It took me four years in the Corps to realize that for fifteen years of my life, all I wanted was to be was a Marine and fight in a war. Now, all I wanted was to be a nasty, civilian, bum, and live on the beach.

That morning we were bussed down to Kadena Air Force Base and boarded a commercial airliner. We were going to make an hour flight to Osaka, Japan, and then a 10 hour flight back to Hawaii. The Corps had a strict uniform policy for travel attire by not allowing Marines to wear their digital camouflage uniform, and since none of us had our Service C uniform (Charlie's, etc.), so they "allowed" us to wear regular, civilian clothes on the plane. Appropriate and serviceable clothing included khaki trousers, a collared shirt, and casual dress shoes.

There was about thirty of us, all with less than 60 days in service left on their contracts. We all intended to get out as soon as we could. Some of us had accrued and saved "leave" days to sell back to the government for a fat check. I had 9 months of tax-free funds stashed in the bank and I wasn't planning to invest it. I had this dream of living in Australia, until I was "Catfished". I thought I could go anywhere and do anything. There was no limit to where I could end up. That was the beauty of being spontaneous and vulnerable. Put your soul on the line and see what evolves. But really, I just wanted to run, for as far and as long as I could before the reality of life and responsibility eventually caught up with me.

As I boarded the 747 jumbo-jet in Osaka, I looked up for my seat in the rows of numbers, increasing farther to the back of economy class. Looking up and down at my ticket while shuffling my feet, and matching the row. I found my seat and right next to me was the most beautiful Japanese girl I had ever seen in my life. She was angelic. I sat down with a smile, but we didn't utter a word. She smiled back, meek and humble. I looked behind me at a few of the guys as they made dick-sucking gestures, prodding their tongue to their cheeks, aided by a hand motion, and then flicking me the middle finger. Yeah I was lucky to sit next to a pretty girl. Every "single" guy hopes for that opportunity on a plane ride. We talked, laughed, and shared music through an IPod. She spoke good English, and said she was moving to Orlando to be with her boyfriend. That was weirdly ominous because that's where I knew I would eventually end up when my lack of a plan, finally fell through. I had some resources there. I lived there for thirteen years, through high school and college.

It seemed plausible that I might see her again, so I left it at that. She fell asleep on my shoulder for the rest of the way. I indulged in the smell of her silky, black hair and my temporary, pseudo-boyfriend status. An early morning sunrise, cresting from the top of Diamond Head, came into view through the plane's porthole window. It was the familiar aerial image of the Honolulu city skyline and the picturesque beaches of Waikiki, with its idyllic backdrop. Slow and low the plane descended. The pilot's expertise smoothly laid the wheels on the deck, with the reassurance of a solid landing. I was completely elated to be back in the Hawaiian Islands. Kaneohe was my place of birth and home until the age of thirteen. There was some mysticism and omnipotence associated with the whole experience. It was that rare and encapsulating moment when life comes "full circle" and I didn't even care that no one knew it was my birthday.

They gave us a hero's welcome. The Marine Corps Band played spirited tunes as familiar faces greeted us at the baggage claim area. A conglomeration, of high ranking, field grade, officers shook my hand and actually offered some reverence, when it usually goes the other way. The humid heat of Honolulu hit my nostrils and I couldn't stop smiling. Newspapers and TV reporters scrambled to the scene of reunited couples and families, interrupting their interlude for an interview, as if anyone could muster the description to verbalize their elation. It was sheer gratitude for their lives on part of the Marines and their families alike. Women held up signs for their husband's with the words "Cold Beer and Hot Chicks". Little boys and girls ran toward their fathers, jumping into their arms, smothering them with hugs, kisses, and tears. It was a captivating and surreal moment. People were hugging me that I had never met before. I saw older gentlemen walking with canes, Vietnam Veterans, waiting to shake our hands and say "Thank You", something so basically human, yet they never received a homecoming. I thought about how much tougher they were than me. I felt guilty for being alive because it felt so damn good.

After the crowd dissipated, the single Marines boarded a bus for Marine Corps Base Hawaii, Kaneohe Bay. Upon entering the gate, we were, again, greeted from a hail of hoots, hollers, and cheers, as people lined the roadway with "Welcome Home" signs and care packages. It was a joyous Homecoming to say the least. When we got back to our assigned barracks at the old Mackey Hall, I was pleasantly surprised to see some of the guys who were wounded and medically evacuated months before. Some had the visible signs of physical trauma. Arms, legs and hands all fucked up and mangled from ferocious firefights. Some guys lost an eye, and most of them were waiting on the long, arduous process of a "medical separation board". It's basically how the military evaluates how disabled you are before they discharge you from service. It can take months and sometimes years of bureaucratic bullshit to finally get out. This is exacerbated by the fact, that the government is required to fulfill certain criteria before they are legally allowed to release a wounded veteran back into civil society. I had saved 45 days of leave time on the books and sold 15 days of it back to the government, which meant I had 30 days terminal leave and 15 remaining days to get my shit together to EAS.

I methodically broke it down to how long it would take me to maneuver my way around to all the various offices and medical assignments, each day, to be done on time. March 31st was my target date for EAS. There were a slew of medical evaluations, including dental. I had a list of about 25 different signatures that I needed to complete to be officially discharged. I had to check out of places that I never even checked into, like the pool, the base library, the bowling alley, legal affairs, and the ever so crucial, career retention office.

When I walked in there to get signed off, they offer you "a last chance to re-enlist" scenario. So I humored the fat, POG Staff Sergeant and asked him what my options were. As I waited for him to tantalize me with a reason to re-enlist, he was sitting at his desk as he scrolled down a stapled list of paper and flipped it a couple of times. "Ummmm, well, I have some slots open in 7th Marines", he murmured. The 7th Marine Regiment was based in 29 Palms, California (affectionately known as "29 Stumps"), absolutely the worst and most avoided duty station within the entire Marine Corps. Located out in the Southern California desert, it was a two hour drive to LA or Las Vegas in either direction with nothing but dust and sand in between. I just chuckled to myself and looked down, thinking "Man, that's definitely not enough to make me reconsider staying another day in this gun club. It must be my destiny to only do four and out". I just lazily shook my head, side to side without even uttering a proper response. He reiterated the new tattoo policy, virtually nullifying any chance of me getting back in, once I got out. Again, I remained undeterred. He scoffed at his inability to be convincing and shuffled me away with the scribble of his pen. My checkout sheet was almost complete.

March 31, 2005 – Commence Terminal Leave

The last remaining signature was by my acting, Company Commander, Capt. Botard. He was a real condescending asshole with large, black, bushy eyebrows. He sat at his desk with his arms crossed, as I respectfully reported into him. "Stand at ease, Corporal. So....you're gonna get out of the Marine Corps and go find yourself, huh"? "Uh, yes sir" I replied. "Yeah and then you're gonna go be some anti-war protesting, hippie, tree-huggin', faggot, huh"? "No sir....four years was enough and I'd like to see what else life has to offer". He just glared at me for a moment. "Alright Corporal, I'm going to sign off on this and you will commence to terminal leave at 1630, today...Good Luck". And just like that, I was out. Free!!!

Cited with an "Honorable Discharge" and with my DD-214 in hand, I lugged around my whole life in two sea bags. After hitching a ride "Downtown" in an "island beater", Honda Civic, I never turned my head for a last look. I just glanced in the broken rearview mirror as K-Bay, MCBH (Marine Corps Base Hawaii) faded from sight. For the next three weeks, I was inebriated and slept on a futon in a high rise, apartment on Waikiki Beach. My autonomy had begun.

Made in the USA
Lexington, KY
17 July 2014